Philips Essential
AIR FRYER
Cookbook UK 2023

Quick & Easy Delicious Recipes for Your Philips Essential Air Fryer

Gabriel Booth

Legal & Disclaimer

The information contained in this book and its contents is not designed to replace or take the place of any form of medical or professional advice; and is not meant to replace the need for independent medical, financial, legal or other professional advice or services, as may be required. The content and information in this book has been provided for educational and entertainment purposes only.

The content and information contained in this book has been compiled from sources deemed reliable, and it is accurate to the best of the Author's knowledge, information and belief. However, the Author cannot guarantee its accuracy and validity and cannot be held liable for any errors and/or omissions. Further, changes are periodically made to this book as and when needed. Where appropriate and/or necessary, you must consult a professional (including but not limited to your doctor, attorney, financial advisor or such other professional advisor) before using any of the suggested remedies, techniques, or information in this book.

CONTENTS

INTRODUCTION

The air fryer is a great tool on its own, but you can kick things up a notch when you use it with some other kitchen utensils you probably already have on hand. One of the dangers of air frying is overcooking the food you're making. With these tips, you'll avoid that problem and air fry like a pro! The air fryer obviously is a great way to prepare food in your kitchen, but have you ever thought about taking it on the road? With these tips, you'll be air frying wherever your wheels take you!

5 KITCHEN TOOLS TO USE WITH YOUR AIR FRYER

Nothing is worse than buying a new appliance that requires you to spend an extra hundred bucks in special gadgets, right? Rest assured, the air fryer does not require you to do that! Using those kitchen tools you already have on hand, your air-fried foods will come to life. And even if you're not a cook and you need to invest in a few of the items listed here, they won't cost you an arm and a leg and you'll find multiple uses for them in your home.

Here are five air-fryer-friendly kitchen tools to have on hand:

- Silicone muffin liners: Make your muffins come to life with silicone muffin liners. Heat stable and perfectly portioned, silicone muffin liners allow you to bring the beauty of breads to the comfort of your own kitchen. Plus, you can even make baked eggs in them.

- Seven-inch springform (Bundt) pan: Cheesecakes and coffee cakes have a seat at your table when you invest in one of these (usually sold as a convertible cake and Bundt cake pan). You can enjoy a bakery-fresh slice of cake for less than a fraction of the cost.

- Seven-inch oven-safe casserole dish: Most air fryers don't exceed 400 degrees, meaning the same small casserole dish that withstands your oven temperatures will be safe in your air fryer, too. From glass to metal to silicone, the air fryer should accommodate them all!

- Metal skewers: Take those skewers from the grill and use them in your air fryer to help evenly cook thicker cuts of meat. Depending on the type of air fryer you have, the skewers may (or may not) be too big for your fryer. If you're on the fence about skewers that will fit your air fryer, you can use wooden sticks (just be cautious of the temperature so you don't catch them on fire).

- Kitchen tongs: Using a pair of kitchen tongs is essential to ensure you don't burn another finger trying to get that last chip that's nestled itself on the side of the fryer basket.

5 WAYS TO PREVENT AIR FRYING YOUR FOOD TO A CRISP

When cooking certain foods at high temperatures, charring can occur. That charring produces a chemical called acrylamide. And acrylamide might be linked to an increased risk of cancer. It's important to note that, according to the American Cancer Society, "It's not yet clear if the levels of acrylamide in foods raise cancer risk." Still, you can take some steps to avoid frying foods to a crisp. **Here's what we recommend:**

- Cook at lower temperatures for longer periods of time (instead of high temperatures for shorter periods). Turning the temperature knob down to 300 to 325 degrees and increasing the time to 10 or 20 minutes may prevent charred coffee cake and blackened fries.

- Cover foods with foil. The air fryer works to cook your foods by circulating air throughout the basket, so you don't want to prevent that air flow. However, you can use foil to cover a chicken breast, for example, and place it in the basket to cook (low and slow). We also suggest using foil to cover cakes and egg dishes to prevent the top from cooking too quickly. Just be sure there is enough room between the foil and the top of the air fryer.

- Don't overfill the basket. You may be tempted to throw the entire batch of beet chips or broccoli florets into the basket at once to save time, but that will result in uneven cooking and a few pieces getting burned to a crisp. Either invest in a larger fryer or cook in smaller batches to produce the perfect air-fried foods every time.

- Use air-fryer-safe equipment. The key to producing bakery-perfect muffins or quick breads lies in making sure you're using the right equipment. Using the right equipment helps allow the air to circulate properly, leaving your air-fried foods crisp, crunchy, and evenly cooked.

- Set timers and reminders. We all need to set alarms to remember important things, and air frying your foods is no different. Set timers not only on your air fryer but on your phone so you don't leave the foods cooking any longer than required.

AIR FRYING ON THE ROAD

If you travel in an RV, you know space is tight. And yet many RVers are adding an air fryer to their tiny kitchens. Why? Because nothing beats an air fryer for reheating food with ease, making your favorite chicken wings without heating up your RV, and enjoying fresh baked cookies after a long day of hiking. But before you pack up, you need to understand the electrical requirements of both your vehicle and your air fryer, so be sure to review your camper's electrical needs first.

When you've determined that your air fryer will work in your vehicle, you're ready to get cooking! The following simple meals will be perfect for your next road trip:

- ♥ Chicken wings: This popular appetizer can be made in the comfort of your RV or camper in 22 minutes! Just season with salt and pepper and cook at 370 degrees for 22 minutes, flipping a couple times. Then finish off with your favorite hot sauce heated up with melted butter. Serve the wings with blue-cheese-stuffed celery, and call it a meal!

- ♥ Steak and potatoes: Who doesn't appreciate a good steak while taking in another stellar sunset? Dice potatoes and season with salt and pepper. Then cook at 360 degrees for 5 minutes. Season the steak with salt and pepper and place it in the air fryer basket next to the potatoes. Spray the food with cooking spray, crank up the heat to 390 degrees, and cook for 12 minutes, flipping the steak and shaking the potatoes after 6 minutes. Let the steak rest for 5 minutes, and serve with a simple salad to complete the meal.

- ♥ Crispy chimichangas: Whether it's for breakfast, lunch, or dinner, a chimichanga is an easy addition to your meal rotation. Try a simple bean and cheese chimichanga by spreading refried beans onto a tortilla, topping with shredded cheese, and rolling up like a sealed burrito. Spray the chimichanga with cooking spray and cook at 360 degrees for 8 to 10 minutes.

- ♥ BLT: Bacon comes out perfectly in an air fryer, without splattering grease all over your living space. Cook the bacon at 390 degrees for 8 to 10 minutes (or how you like it). Remove the bacon onto a paper towel. Then brush your bread with mayo and place it in the basket. Cook at 370 degrees for 2 minutes. Top with lettuce, tomato, and crispy bacon for a warm lunch!

- ♥ Frozen pizzas: Oh yes, that's right! You can now pick up your favorite frozen fare — from pizzas to Hot Pockets — at a grocery store instead of waiting in line at a restaurant. Be sure to pick up the individual sizes. Whip up a salad from a bag to complete the meal.

BREAD AND BR

Oat Bran Muffins

Servings: 8 / Cooking Time: 12 Mins.

Ingredients:

- ⅔ C. oat bran
- ½ C. flour
- ¼ C. brown sugar
- 1 tsp. baking powder
- ½ tsp. baking soda
- ⅛ tsp. salt
- ½ C. buttermilk
- 1 egg
- 2 tbsp. canola oil
- ½ C. chopped dates, raisins, or dried cranberries
- 24 paper muffin cups
- cooking spray

Directions:

1. Preheat air fryer to 330°F.
2. In a large bowl, combine the oat bran, flour, brown sugar, baking powder, baking soda, and salt.
3. In a small bowl, beat together the buttermilk, egg, and oil.
4. Pour buttermilk mixture into bowl with dry ingredients and stir just until moistened. Do not beat.
5. Gently stir in dried fruit.
6. Use triple baking C. to help muffins hold shape during baking. Spray them with cooking spray, place 4 sets of C. in air fryer basket at a time, and fill each one ¾ full of batter.
7. Cook for 12minutes, until top springs back when lightly touched and toothpick inserted in center comes out clean.
8. Repeat for remaining muffins.

Not-so-english Muffins

Servings: 4 / Cooking Time: 10 Mins.

Ingredients:

- 2 strips turkey bacon, cut in half crosswise
- 2 whole-grain English muffins, split
- 1 C. fresh baby spinach, long stems removed
- ¼ ripe pear, peeled and thinly sliced
- 4 slices Provolone cheese

Directions:

1. Place bacon strips in air fryer basket and cook for 2minutes. Check and separate strips if necessary so they cook evenly. Cook for 4 more minutes, until crispy. Remove and drain on paper towels.
2. Place split muffin halves in air fryer basket and cook at 390°F for 2minutes, just until lightly browned.
3. Open air fryer and top each muffin with a quarter of the baby spinach, several pear slices, a strip of bacon, and a slice of cheese.
4. Cook at 360°F for 2minutes, until cheese completely melts.

Sweet Potato-cinnamon Toast

Servings: 6 / Cooking Time: 8 Mins.

Ingredients:

- 1 small sweet potato, cut into ⅜-inch slices
- oil for misting
- ground cinnamon

Directions:

1. Preheat air fryer to 390°F.
2. Spray both sides of sweet potato slices with oil. Sprinkle both sides with cinnamon to taste.
3. Place potato slices in air fryer basket in a single layer.
4. Cook for 4minutes, turn, and cook for 4 more minutes or until potato slices are barely fork tender.

Pancake Muffins

Servings: 4 / Cooking Time: 8 Mins.

Ingredients:

- 1 C. flour
- 2 tbsp. sugar (optional)
- ½ tsp. baking soda
- 1 tsp. baking powder
- ¼ tsp. salt
- 1 egg, beaten
- 1 C. buttermilk
- 2 tbsp. melted butter
- 1 tsp. pure vanilla extract
- 24 foil muffin cups
- cooking spray
- Suggested Fillings
- 1 tsp. of jelly or fruit preserves
- 1 tbsp. or less fresh blueberries; chopped fresh strawberries; chopped frozen cherries; dark chocolate chips; chopped walnuts, pecans, or other nuts; cooked, crumbled bacon or sausage

Directions:

1. In a large bowl, stir together flour, optional sugar, baking soda, baking powder, and salt.
2. In a small bowl, combine egg, buttermilk, butter, and vanilla. Mix well.
3. Pour egg mixture into dry ingredients and stir to mix well but don't overbeat.
4. Double up the muffin C. and remove the paper liners from the top cups. Spray the foil C. lightly with cooking spray.
5. Place 6 sets of muffin C. in air fryer basket. Pour just enough batter into each C. to cover the bottom. Sprinkle with desired filling. Pour in more batter to cover the filling and fill the C. about ¾ full.
6. Cook at 330°F for 8minutes.
7. Repeat steps 5 and 6 for the remaining 6 pancake muffins.

Cheesy Olive And Roasted Pepper Bread

Servings: 8 / Cooking Time: 7 Mins.

Ingredients:

- 7-inch round bread boule
- olive oil
- ½ C. mayonnaise
- 2 tbsp. butter, melted
- 1 C. grated mozzarella or Fontina cheese
- ¼ C. grated Parmesan cheese
- ½ tsp. dried oregano
- ½ C. black olives, sliced
- ½ C. green olives, sliced
- ½ C. coarsely chopped roasted red peppers
- 2 tbsp. minced red onion
- freshly ground black pepper

Directions:

1. Preheat the air fryer to 370°F.
2. Cut the bread boule in half horizontally. If your bread boule has a rounded top, trim the top of the boule so that the top half will lie flat with the cut side facing up. Lightly brush both sides of the boule halves with olive oil.
3. Place one half of the boule into the air fryer basket with the center cut side facing down. Air-fry at 370°F for 2 minutes to lightly toast the bread. Repeat with the other half of the bread boule.
4. Combine the mayonnaise, butter, mozzarella cheese, Parmesan cheese and dried oregano in a small bowl. Fold in the black and green olives, roasted red peppers and red onion and season with freshly ground black pepper. Spread the cheese mixture over the untoasted side of the bread, covering the entire surface.
5. Air-fry at 350°F for 5 minutes until the cheese is melted and browned. Repeat with the other half. Cut into slices and serve warm.

All-in-one Breakfast Toast

Servings: 1 / Cooking Time: 10 Mins.

Ingredients:

- 1 strip of bacon, diced
- 1 slice of 1-inch thick bread (such as Texas Toast or hand-sliced bread)
- 1 tbsp. softened butter (optional)
- 1 egg
- salt and freshly ground black pepper
- ¼ C. grated Colby or Jack cheese

Directions:

1. Preheat the air fryer to 400°F.
2. Air-fry the bacon for 3 minutes, shaking the basket once or twice while it cooks. Remove the bacon to a paper towel lined plate and set aside.
3. Use a sharp paring knife to score a large circle in the middle of the slice of bread, cutting halfway through, but not all the way through to the cutting board. Press down on the circle in the center of the bread slice to create an indentation. If using, spread the softened butter on the edges and in the hole of the bread.
4. Transfer the slice of bread, hole side up, to the air fryer basket. Crack the egg into the center of the bread, and season with salt and pepper.
5. Air-fry at 380°F for 5 minutes. Sprinkle the grated cheese around the edges of the bread leaving the center of the yolk uncovered, and top with the cooked bacon. Press the cheese and bacon into the bread lightly to help anchor it to the bread and prevent it from blowing around in the air fryer.
6. Air-fry for one or two more minutes (depending on how you like your egg cooked), just to melt the cheese and finish cooking the egg. Serve immediately.

Cheddar-ham-corn Muffins

Servings: 8 / Cooking Time: 8 Mins.

Ingredients:

- ¾ C. yellow cornmeal
- ¼ C. flour
- 1½ tsp. baking powder
- ¼ tsp. salt
- 1 egg, beaten
- 2 tbsp. canola oil
- ½ C. milk
- ½ C. shredded sharp Cheddar cheese
- ½ C. diced ham
- 8 foil muffin cups, liners removed and sprayed with cooking spray

Directions:

1. Preheat air fryer to 390°F.
2. In a medium bowl, stir together the cornmeal, flour, baking powder, and salt.
3. Add egg, oil, and milk to dry ingredients and mix well.
4. Stir in shredded cheese and diced ham.
5. Divide batter among the muffin cups.
6. Place 4 filled muffin C. in air fryer basket and bake for 5minutes.
7. Reduce temperature to 330°F and bake for 1 to 2minutes or until toothpick inserted in center of muffin comes out clean.
8. Repeat steps 6 and 7 to cook remaining muffins.

Cinnamon Sugar Donut Holes

Servings: 12 / Cooking Time: 6 Mins.

Ingredients:

- 1 C. all-purpose flour
- 6 tbsp. cane sugar, divided
- 1 tsp. baking powder
- 3 tsp. ground cinnamon, divided
- ¼ tsp. salt
- 1 large egg
- 1 tsp. vanilla extract
- 2 tbsp. melted butter

Directions:

1. Preheat the air fryer to 370°F.
2. In a small bowl, combine the flour, 2 tbsp. of the sugar, the baking powder, 1 tsp. of the cinnamon, and the salt. Mix well.
3. In a larger bowl, whisk together the egg, vanilla extract, and butter.
4. Slowly add the dry ingredients into the wet until all the ingredients are uniformly combined. Set the bowl inside the refrigerator for at least 30 minutes.
5. Before you're ready to cook, in a small bowl, mix together the remaining 4 tbsp. of sugar and 2 tsp. of cinnamon.
6. Liberally spray the air fryer basket with olive oil mist so the donut holes don't stick to the bottom. Note: You do not want to use parchment paper in this recipe; it may burn if your air fryer is hotter than others.
7. Remove the dough from the refrigerator and divide it into 12 equal donut holes. You can use a 1-ounce serving scoop if you have one.
8. Roll each donut hole in the sugar and cinnamon mixture; then place in the air fryer basket. Repeat until all the donut holes are covered in the sugar and cinnamon mixture.
9. When the basket is full, cook for 6 minutes. Remove the donut holes from the basket using oven-safe tongs and let cool 5 minutes. Repeat until all 12 are cooked.

Southern Sweet Cornbread

Servings: 6 / Cooking Time: 17 Mins.

Ingredients:

- cooking spray
- ½ C. white cornmeal
- ½ C. flour
- 2 tsp. baking powder
- ½ tsp. salt
- 4 tsp. sugar
- 1 egg
- 2 tbsp. oil
- ½ C. milk

Directions:

1. Preheat air fryer to 360°F.
2. Spray air fryer baking pan with nonstick cooking spray.
3. In a medium bowl, stir together the cornmeal, flour, baking powder, salt, and sugar.
4. In a small bowl, beat together the egg, oil, and milk. Stir into dry ingredients until well combined.
5. Pour batter into prepared baking pan.
6. Cook at 360°F for 17 minutes or until toothpick inserted in center comes out clean or with crumbs clinging.

Quesadillas

Servings: 4 / Cooking Time: 12 Mins.

Ingredients:

- 4 eggs
- 2 tbsp. skim milk
- salt and pepper
- oil for misting or cooking spray
- 4 flour tortillas
- 4 tbsp. salsa
- 2 oz. Cheddar cheese, grated
- ½ small avocado, peeled and thinly sliced

Directions:

1. Preheat air fryer to 270°F.
2. Beat together eggs, milk, salt, and pepper.
3. Spray a 6 x 6-inch air fryer baking pan lightly with cooking spray and add egg mixture.
4. Cook 9minutes, stirring every 1 to 2minutes, until eggs are scrambled to your liking. Remove and set aside.
5. Spray one side of each tortilla with oil or cooking spray. Flip over.
6. Divide eggs, salsa, cheese, and avocado among the tortillas, covering only half of each tortilla.
7. Fold each tortilla in half and press down lightly.
8. Place 2 tortillas in air fryer basket and cook at 390°F for 3minutes or until cheese melts and outside feels slightly crispy. Repeat with remaining two tortillas.
9. Cut each cooked tortilla into halves or thirds.

Pepperoni Pizza Bread

Servings: 4 / Cooking Time: 15 Mins.

Ingredients:

- 7-inch round bread boule
- 2 C. grated mozzarella cheese
- 1 tbsp. dried oregano
- 1 C. pizza sauce
- 1 C. mini pepperoni or pepperoni slices, cut in quarters
- Pizza sauce for dipping (optional)

Directions:

1. Make 7 to 8 deep slices across the bread boule, leaving 1 inch of bread uncut at the bottom of every slice before you reach the cutting board. The slices should go about three quarters of the way through the boule and be about 2 inches apart from each other. Turn the bread boule 90 degrees and make 7 to 8 similar slices perpendicular to the first slices to form squares in the bread. Again, make sure you don't cut all the way through the bread.
2. Combine the mozzarella cheese and oregano in a small bowl.
3. Fill the slices in the bread with pizza sauce by gently spreading the bread apart and spooning the sauce in between the squares of bread. Top the sauce with the mozzarella cheese mixture and then the pepperoni. Do your very best to get the cheese and pepperoni in between the slices, rather than on top of the bread. Keep spreading the bread apart and stuffing the ingredients in, but be careful not to tear the bottom of the bread.
4. Preheat the air fryer to 320°F.
5. Transfer the bread boule to the air fryer basket and air-fry for 15 minutes, making sure the top doesn't get too dark. (It will just be the cheese on top that gets dark, so if you've done a good job of tucking the cheese in between the slices, this shouldn't be an issue.)
6. Carefully remove the bread from the basket with a spatula. Transfer it to a serving platter with more sauce to dip into if desired. Serve with a lot of napkins so that people can just pull the bread apart with their hands and enjoy!

Carrot Orange Muffins

Servings: 12 / Cooking Time: 12 Mins.

Ingredients:

- 1½ C. all-purpose flour
- ½ C. granulated sugar
- ½ tsp. ground cinnamon
- 2 tsp. baking powder
- ¼ tsp. baking soda
- ½ tsp. salt
- 2 large eggs
- ¼ C. vegetable oil
- ⅓ C. orange marmalade
- 2 C. grated carrots

Directions:

1. Preheat the air fryer to 320°F.
2. In a large bowl, whisk together the flour, sugar, cinnamon, baking powder, baking soda, and salt; set aside.
3. In a separate bowl, whisk together the eggs, vegetable oil, orange marmalade, and grated carrots.
4. Make a well in the dry ingredients; then pour the wet ingredients into the well of the dry ingredients. Using a rubber spatula, mix the ingredients for 1 minute or until slightly lumpy.
5. Using silicone muffin liners, fill 6 muffin liners two-thirds full.
6. Carefully place the muffin liners in the air fryer basket and bake for 12 minutes (or until the tops are browned and a toothpick inserted in the center comes out clean). Carefully remove the muffins from the basket and repeat with remaining batter.
7. Serve warm.

DESSERTS AND SWEETS

Struffoli

Servings: x / Cooking Time: 20 Mins.

Ingredients:

- ¼ C. butter, softened
- ⅔ C. sugar
- 5 eggs
- 2 tsp. vanilla extract
- zest of 1 lemon
- 4 C. all-purpose flour
- 2 tsp. baking soda
- ¼ tsp. salt
- 16 oz. honey
- 1 tsp. ground cinnamon
- zest of 1 orange
- 2 tbsp. water
- nonpareils candy sprinkles

Directions:

1. Cream the butter and sugar together in a bowl until light and fluffy using a hand mixer (or a stand mixer). Add the eggs, vanilla and lemon zest and mix. In a separate bowl, combine the flour, baking soda and salt. Add the dry ingredients to the wet ingredients and mix until you have a soft dough. Shape the dough into a ball, wrap it in plastic and let it rest for 30 minutes.
2. Divide the dough ball into four pieces. Roll each piece into a long rope. Cut each rope into about 25 (½-inch) pieces. Roll each piece into a tight ball. You should have 100 little balls when finished.
3. Preheat the air fryer to 370°F.
4. In batches of about 20, transfer the dough balls to the air fryer basket, leaving a small space in between them. Air-fry the dough balls at 370°F for 3 to 4 minutes, shaking the basket when one minute of cooking time remains.
5. After all the dough balls are air-fried, make the honey topping. Melt the honey in a small saucepan on the stovetop. Add the cinnamon, orange zest, and water. Simmer for one minute. Place the air-fried dough balls in a large bowl and drizzle the honey mixture over top. Gently toss to coat all the dough balls evenly. Transfer the coated struffoli to a platter and sprinkle the nonpareil candy sprinkles over top. You can dress the presentation up by piling the balls into the shape of a wreath or pile them high in a cone shape to resemble a Christmas tree.
6. Struffoli can be made ahead. Store covered tightly.

Vegan Brownie Bites

Servings: 10 / Cooking Time: 8 Mins.

Ingredients:

- ⅔ C. walnuts
- ⅓ C. all-purpose flour
- ¼ C. dark cocoa powder
- ⅓ C. cane sugar
- ¼ tsp. salt
- 2 tbsp. vegetable oil
- 1 tsp. pure vanilla extract
- 1 tbsp. almond milk
- 1 tbsp. powdered sugar

Directions:

1. Preheat the air fryer to 350°F.
2. To a blender or food processor fitted with a metal blade, add the walnuts, flour, cocoa powder, sugar, and salt. Pulse until smooth, about 30 seconds. Add in the oil, vanilla, and milk and pulse until a dough is formed.
3. Remove the dough and place in a bowl. Form into 10 equal-size bites.
4. Liberally spray the metal trivet in the air fryer basket with olive oil mist. Place the brownie bites into the basket and cook for 8 minutes, or until the outer edges begin to slightly crack.
5. Remove the basket from the air fryer and let cool. Sprinkle the brownie bites with powdered sugar and serve.

One-bowl Chocolate Buttermilk Cake

Servings: 6 / Cooking Time: 16-20 Mins.

Ingredients:

- ¾ C. All-purpose flour
- ½ C. Granulated white sugar
- 3 tbsp. Unsweetened cocoa powder
- ½ tsp. Baking soda
- ¼ tsp. Table salt
- ½ C. Buttermilk
- 2 tbsp. Vegetable oil
- ¾ tsp. Vanilla extract
- Baking spray (see here)

Directions:

1. Preheat the air fryer to 325°F (or 330°F, if that's the closest setting).
2. Stir the flour, sugar, cocoa powder, baking soda, and salt in a large bowl until well combined. Add the buttermilk, oil, and vanilla. Stir just until a thick, grainy batter forms.
3. Use the baking spray to generously coat the inside of a 6-inch round cake pan for a small batch, a 7-inch round cake pan for a medium batch, or an 8-inch round cake pan for a large batch. Scrape and spread the chocolate batter into this pan, smoothing the batter out to an even layer.
4. Set the pan in the basket and air-fry undisturbed for 16 minutes for a 6-inch layer, 18 minutes for a 7-inch layer, or 20 minutes for an 8-inch layer, or until a toothpick or cake tester inserted into the center of the cake comes out clean. Start checking it at the 14-minute mark to know where you are.
5. Use hot pads or silicone baking mitts to transfer the cake pan to a wire rack. Cool for 5 minutes. To unmold, set a cutting board over the baking pan and invert both the board and the pan. Lift the still-warm pan off the cake layer. Set the wire rack on top of the cake layer and invert all of it with the cutting board so that the cake layer is now right side up on the wire rack. Remove the cutting board and continue cooling the cake for at least 10 minutes or to room temperature, about 30 minutes, before slicing into wedges.

Oreo-coated Peanut Butter Cups

Servings: 8 / Cooking Time: 4 Mins.

Ingredients:

- 8 Standard ¾-ounce peanut butter cups, frozen
- ⅓ C. All-purpose flour
- 2 Large egg white(s), beaten until foamy
- 16 Oreos or other creme-filled chocolate sandwich cookies, ground to crumbs in a food processor
- Vegetable oil spray

Directions:

1. Set up and fill three shallow soup plates or small pie plates on your counter: one for the flour, one for the beaten egg white(s), and one for the cookie crumbs.
2. Dip a frozen peanut butter C. in the flour, turning it to coat all sides. Shake off any excess, then set it in the beaten egg white(s). Turn it to coat all sides, then let any excess egg white slip back into the rest. Set the candy bar in the cookie crumbs. Turn to coat on all parts, even the sides. Dip the peanut butter C. back in the egg white(s) as before, then into the cookie crumbs as before, making sure you have a solid, even coating all around the cup. Set aside while you dip and coat the remaining cups.
3. When all the peanut butter C. are dipped and coated, lightly coat them on all sides with the vegetable oil spray. Set them on a plate and freeze while the air fryer heats.
4. Preheat the air fryer to 400°F.
5. Set the dipped C. wider side up in the basket with as much air space between them as possible. Air-fry undisturbed for 4 minutes, or until they feel soft but the coating is set.
6. Turn off the machine and remove the basket from it. Set aside the basket with the fried C. for 10 minutes. Use a nonstick-safe spatula to transfer the fried C. to a wire rack. Cool for at least another 5 minutes before serving.

Pear And Almond Biscotti Crumble

Servings: 6 / Cooking Time: 65 Mins.

Ingredients:

- 7-inch cake pan or ceramic dish
- 3 pears, peeled, cored and sliced
- ½ C. brown sugar
- ¼ tsp. ground ginger
- 1 tsp. ground cinnamon
- ⅛ tsp. ground nutmeg
- 2 tbsp. cornstarch
- 1¼ C. (4 to 5) almond biscotti, coarsely crushed
- ¼ C. all-purpose flour
- ¼ C. sliced almonds
- ¼ C. butter, melted

Directions:

1. Combine the pears, brown sugar, ginger, cinnamon, nutmeg and cornstarch in a bowl. Toss to combine and then pour the pear mixture into a greased 7-inch cake pan or ceramic dish.
2. Combine the crushed biscotti, flour, almonds and melted butter in a medium bowl. Toss with a fork until the mixture resembles large crumbles. Sprinkle the biscotti crumble over the pears and cover the pan with aluminum foil.
3. Preheat the air fryer to 350°F.
4. Air-fry at 350°F for 60 minutes. Remove the aluminum foil and air-fry for an additional 5 minutes to brown the crumble layer.
5. Serve warm.

Giant Oatmeal–peanut Butter Cookie

Servings: 4 / Cooking Time: 18 Mins.

Ingredients:

- 1 C. Rolled oats (not quick-cooking or steel-cut oats)
- ½ C. All-purpose flour
- ½ tsp. Ground cinnamon
- ½ tsp. Baking soda
- ⅓ C. Packed light brown sugar
- ¼ C. Solid vegetable shortening
- 2 tbsp. Natural-style creamy peanut butter
- 3 tbsp. Granulated white sugar
- 2 tbsp. (or 1 small egg, well beaten) Pasteurized egg substitute, such as Egg Beaters
- ⅓ C. Roasted, salted peanuts, chopped
- Baking spray

Directions:

1. Preheat the air fryer to 350°F.
2. Stir the oats, flour, cinnamon, and baking soda in a bowl until well combined.
3. Using an electric hand mixer at medium speed, beat the brown sugar, shortening, peanut butter, granulated white sugar, and egg substitute or egg (as applicable) until smooth and creamy, about 3 minutes, scraping down the inside of the bowl occasionally.
4. Scrape down and remove the beaters. Fold in the flour mixture and peanuts with a rubber spatula just until all the flour is moistened and the peanut bits are evenly distributed in the dough.
5. For a small air fryer, coat the inside of a 6-inch round cake pan with baking spray. For a medium air fryer, coat the inside of a 7-inch round cake pan with baking spray. And for a large air fryer, coat the inside of an 8-inch round cake pan with baking spray. Scrape and gently press the dough into the prepared pan, spreading it into an even layer to the perimeter.
6. Set the pan in the basket and air-fry undisturbed for 18 minutes, or until well browned.
7. Transfer the pan to a wire rack and cool for 15 minutes. Loosen the cookie from the perimeter with a spatula, then invert the pan onto a cutting board and let the cookie come free. Remove the pan and reinvert the cookie onto the wire rack. Cool for 5 minutes more before slicing into wedges to serve.

Coconut Crusted Bananas With Pineapple Sauce

Servings: 4 / Cooking Time: 5 Mins.

Ingredients:

- Pineapple Sauce
- 1½ C. puréed fresh pineapple
- 2 tbsp. sugar
- juice of 1 lemon
- ¼ tsp. ground cinnamon
- 3 firm bananas
- ¼ C. sweetened condensed milk
- 1¼ C. shredded coconut
- ⅓ C. crushed graham crackers (crumbs)*
- vegetable or canola oil, in a spray bottle
- vanilla frozen yogurt or ice cream

Directions:

1. Make the pineapple sauce by combining the pineapple, sugar, lemon juice and cinnamon in a saucepan. Simmer the mixture on the stovetop for 20 minutes, and then set it aside.
2. Slice the bananas diagonally into ½-inch thick slices and place them in a bowl. Pour the sweetened condensed milk into the bowl and toss the bananas gently to coat. Combine the coconut and graham cracker crumbs together in a shallow dish. Remove the banana slices from the condensed milk and let any excess milk drip off. Dip the banana slices in the coconut and crumb mixture to coat both sides. Spray the coated slices with oil.
3. Preheat the air fryer to 400°F.
4. Grease the bottom of the air fryer basket with a little oil. Air-fry the bananas in batches at 400°F for 5 minutes, turning them over halfway through the cooking time. Air-fry until the bananas are golden brown on both sides.
5. Serve warm over vanilla frozen yogurt with some of the pineapple sauce spooned over top.

Banana Bread Cake

Servings: 6 / Cooking Time: 18-22 Mins.

Ingredients:

- ¾ C. plus 2 tbsp. All-purpose flour
- ½ tsp. Baking powder
- ¼ tsp. Baking soda
- ¼ tsp. Table salt
- 4 tbsp. (¼ cup/½ stick) Butter, at room temperature
- ½ C. Granulated white sugar
- 2 Small ripe bananas, peeled
- 5 tbsp. Pasteurized egg substitute, such as Egg Beaters
- ¼ C. Buttermilk
- ¾ tsp. Vanilla extract
- Baking spray (see here)

Directions:

1. Preheat the air fryer to 325°F (or 330°F, if that's the closest setting).
2. Mix the flour, baking powder, baking soda, and salt in a small bowl until well combined.
3. Using an electric hand mixer at medium speed, beat the butter and sugar in a medium bowl until creamy and smooth, about 3 minutes, occasionally scraping down the inside of the bowl.
4. Beat in the bananas until smooth. Then beat in egg substitute or egg, buttermilk, and vanilla until uniform. (The batter may look curdled at this stage. The flour mixture will smooth it out.) Add the flour mixture and beat at low speed until smooth and creamy.
5. Use the baking spray to generously coat the inside of a 6-inch round cake pan for a small batch, a 7-inch round cake pan for a medium batch, or an 8-inch round cake pan for a large batch. Scrape and spread the batter into the pan, smoothing the batter out to an even layer.
6. Set the pan in the basket and air-fry for 18 minutes for a 6-inch layer, 20 minutes for a 7-inch layer, or 22 minutes for an 8-inch layer, or until the cake is well browned and set even if there's a little soft give right at the center. Start checking it at the 16-minute mark to know where you are.
7. Use hot pads or silicone baking mitts to transfer the cake pan to a wire rack. To unmold, set a cutting board over the baking pan and invert both the board and the pan. Lift the still-warm pan off the cake layer. Set the wire rack on top of that layer and invert all of it with the cutting board so that the cake layer is now right side up on the wire rack. Remove the cutting board and continue cooling the cake for at least 10 minutes or to room temperature, about 40 minutes, before slicing into wedges.

Wild Blueberry Sweet Empanadas

Servings: 12 / Cooking Time: 8 Mins.

Ingredients:

- 2 C. frozen wild blueberries
- 5 tbsp. chia seeds
- ¼ C. honey
- 1 tbsp. lemon or lime juice
- ¼ C. water
- 1½ C. all-purpose flour
- 1 C. whole-wheat flour
- ½ tsp. salt
- 1 tbsp. sugar
- ½ C. cold unsalted butter
- 1 egg
- ½ C. plus 2 tbsp. milk, divided
- 1 C. powdered sugar
- 1 tsp. vanilla extract

Directions:

1. To make the wild blueberry chia jam, place the blueberries, chia seeds, honey, lemon or lime juice, and water into a blender and pulse for 2 minutes. Pour the chia jam into a glass jar or bowl and cover. Store in the refrigerator at least 4 to 8 hours or until the jam is thickened.
2. In a food processor, place the all-purpose flour, whole-wheat flour, salt, sugar, and butter and process for 2 minutes, scraping down the sides of the food processor every 30 seconds. Add in the egg and blend for 30 seconds. Using the pulse button, add in ½ C. of the milk 1 tbsp. at a time or until the dough is moist enough to handle and be rolled into a ball. Let the dough rest at room temperature for 30 minutes.
3. On a floured surface, cut the dough in half; then form a ball and cut each ball into 6 equal pieces, totaling 12 equal pieces. Work with one piece at a time, and cover the remaining dough with a towel. Roll out the dough into a 6-inch round, much like a tortilla, with ¼ inch thickness. Place 4 tbsp. of filling in the center of round, fold over to form a half-circle. Using a fork, crimp the edges together and pierce the top with a fork for air holes. Repeat with the remaining dough and filling.
4. Preheat the air fryer to 350°F.
5. Working in batches, place 3 to 4 empanadas in the air fryer basket and spray with cooking spray. Cook for 8 minutes. Repeat in batches, as needed. Allow the sweet empanadas to cool for 15 minutes. Meanwhile, in a small bowl, whisk together the powdered sugar, the remaining 2 tbsp. of milk, and the vanilla extract. Then drizzle the glaze over the surface and serve.

Sugared Pizza Dough Dippers With Raspberry Cream Cheese Dip

Servings: 10 / Cooking Time: 8 Mins.

Ingredients:

- 1 lb. pizza dough*
- ½ C. butter, melted
- ¾ to 1 C. sugar
- Raspberry Cream Cheese Dip
- 4 oz. cream cheese, softened
- 2 tbsp. powdered sugar
- ½ tsp. almond extract or almond paste
- 1½ tbsp. milk
- ¼ C. raspberry preserves
- fresh raspberries

Directions:

1. Cut the ingredients in half or save half of the dough for another recipe.
2. When you're ready to make your sugared dough dippers, remove your pizza dough from the refrigerator at least 1 hour prior to baking and let it sit on the counter, covered gently with plastic wrap.
3. Roll the dough into two 15-inch logs. Cut each log into 20 slices and roll each slice so that it is 3- to 3½-inches long. Cut each slice in half and twist the dough halves together 3 to 4 times. Place the twisted dough on a cookie sheet, brush with melted butter and sprinkle sugar over the dough twists.
4. Preheat the air fryer to 350°F.
5. Brush the bottom of the air fryer basket with a little melted butter. Air-fry the dough twists in batches. Place 8 to 12 (depending on the size of your air fryer) in the air fryer basket.
6. Air-fry for 6 minutes. Turn the dough strips over and brush the other side with butter. Air-fry for an additional 2 minutes.
7. While the dough twists are cooking, make the cream cheese and raspberry dip. Whip the cream cheese with a hand mixer until fluffy. Add the powdered sugar, almond extract and milk, and beat until smooth. Fold in the raspberry preserves and transfer to a serving dish.
8. As the batches of dough twists are complete, place them into a shallow dish. Brush with more melted butter and generously coat with sugar, shaking the dish to cover both sides. Serve the sugared dough dippers warm with the raspberry cream cheese dip on the side. Garnish with fresh raspberries.

Orange Gooey Butter Cake

Servings: 6 / Cooking Time: 85 Mins.

Ingredients:

- Crust Layer:
- ½ C. flour
- ¼ C. sugar
- ½ tsp. baking powder
- ⅛ tsp. salt
- 2 oz. (½ stick) unsalted European style butter, melted
- 1 egg
- 1 tsp. orange extract
- 2 tbsp. orange zest
- Gooey Butter Layer:
- 8 oz. cream cheese, softened
- 4 oz. (1 stick) unsalted European style butter, melted
- 2 eggs
- 2 tsp. orange extract
- 2 tbsp. orange zest
- 4 C. powdered sugar
- Garnish:
- powdered sugar
- orange slices

Directions:

1. Preheat the air fryer to 350°F.
2. Grease a 7-inch cake pan and line the bottom with parchment paper. Combine the flour, sugar, baking powder and salt in a bowl. Add the melted butter, egg, orange extract and orange zest. Mix well and press this mixture into the bottom of the greased cake pan. Lower the pan into the basket using an aluminum foil sling (fold a piece of aluminum foil into a strip about 2-inches wide by 24-inches long). Fold the ends of the aluminum foil over the top of the dish before returning the basket to the air fryer. Air-fry uncovered for 8 minutes.
3. To make the gooey butter layer, beat the cream cheese, melted butter, eggs, orange extract and orange zest in a large bowl using an electric hand mixer. Add the powdered sugar in stages, beat until smooth with each addition. Pour this mixture on top of the baked crust in the cake pan. Wrap the pan with a piece of greased aluminum foil, tenting the top of the foil to leave a little room for the cake to rise.
4. Air-fry for 60 minutes at 350°F. Remove the aluminum foil and air-fry for an additional 17 minutes.
5. Let the cake cool inside the pan for at least 10 minutes. Then, run a butter knife around the cake and let the cake cool completely in the pan. When cooled, run the butter knife around the edges of the cake again and invert it onto a plate and then back onto a serving platter. Sprinkle the powdered sugar over the top of the cake and garnish with orange slices.

POULTRY RECIPES

Jerk Chicken Drumsticks

Servings: 2 / Cooking Time: 20 Mins.

Ingredients:

- 1 or 2 cloves garlic
- 1 inch of fresh ginger
- 2 serrano peppers, (with seeds if you like it spicy, seeds removed for less heat)
- 1 tsp. ground allspice
- 1 tsp. ground nutmeg
- 1 tsp. chili powder
- ½ tsp. dried thyme
- ½ tsp. ground cinnamon
- ½ tsp. paprika
- 1 tbsp. brown sugar
- 1 tsp. soy sauce
- 2 tbsp. vegetable oil
- 6 skinless chicken drumsticks

Directions:

1. Combine all the ingredients except the chicken in a small chopper or blender and blend to a paste. Make slashes into the meat of the chicken drumsticks and rub the spice blend all over the chicken (a pair of plastic gloves makes this really easy). Transfer the rubbed chicken to a non-reactive covered container and let the chicken marinate for at least 30 minutes or overnight in the refrigerator.
2. Preheat the air fryer to 400°F.
3. Transfer the drumsticks to the air fryer basket. Air-fry for 10 minutes. Turn the drumsticks over and air-fry for another 10 minutes. Serve warm with some rice and vegetables or a green salad.

Southern-style Chicken Legs

Servings: 6 / Cooking Time: 20 Mins.

Ingredients:

- 2 C. buttermilk
- 1 tbsp. hot sauce
- 12 chicken legs
- ½ tsp. salt
- ½ tsp. pepper
- 1 tsp. paprika
- ½ tsp. onion powder
- 1 tsp. garlic powder
- 1 C. all-purpose flour

Directions:

1. In an airtight container, place the buttermilk, hot sauce, and chicken legs and refrigerate for 4 to 8 hours.
2. In a medium bowl, whisk together the salt, pepper, paprika, onion powder, garlic powder, and flour. Drain the chicken legs from the buttermilk and dip the chicken legs into the flour mixture, stirring to coat well.
3. Preheat the air fryer to 390°F.
4. Place the chicken legs in the air fryer basket and spray with cooking spray. Cook for 10 minutes, turn the chicken legs over, and cook for another 8 to 10 minutes. Check for an internal temperature of 165°F.

Honey Lemon Thyme Glazed Cornish Hen

Servings: 2 / Cooking Time: 20 Mins.

Ingredients:

- 1 (2-pound) Cornish game hen, split in half
- olive oil
- salt and freshly ground black pepper
- ¼ tsp. dried thyme
- ¼ C. honey
- 1 tbsp. lemon zest
- juice of 1 lemon
- 1½ tsp. chopped fresh thyme leaves
- ½ tsp. soy sauce
- freshly ground black pepper

Directions:

1. Split the game hen in half by cutting down each side of the backbone and then cutting through the breast. Brush or spray both halves of the game hen with the olive oil and then season with the salt, pepper and dried thyme.
2. Preheat the air fryer to 390°F.
3. Place the game hen, skin side down, into the air fryer and air-fry for 5 minutes. Turn the hen halves over and air-fry for 10 minutes.
4. While the hen is cooking, combine the honey, lemon zest and juice, fresh thyme, soy sauce and pepper in a small bowl.
5. When the air fryer timer rings, brush the honey glaze onto the game hen and continue to air-fry for another 3 to 5 minutes, just until the hen is nicely glazed, browned and has an internal temperature of 165°F.
6. Let the hen rest for 5 minutes and serve warm.

Chicken Fried Steak With Gravy

Servings: 4 / Cooking Time: 10 Minutes

Ingredients:

- ½ C. flour
- 2 tsp. salt, divided
- freshly ground black pepper
- ¼ tsp. garlic powder
- 1 C. buttermilk
- 1 C. fine breadcrumbs
- 4 tenderized top round steaks (about 6 to 8 oz. each; ½-inch thick)
- vegetable or canola oil
- For the Gravy:
- 2 tbsp. butter or bacon drippings
- ¼ onion, minced (about ¼ cup)
- 1 clove garlic, smashed
- ¼ tsp. dried thyme
- 3 tbsp. flour
- 1 C. milk
- salt and lots of freshly ground black pepper
- a few dashes of Worcestershire sauce

Directions:

1. Set up a dredging station. Combine the flour, 1 tsp. of salt, black pepper and garlic powder in a shallow bowl. Pour the buttermilk into a second shallow bowl. Finally, put the breadcrumbs and 1 tsp. of salt in a third shallow bowl.
2. Dip the tenderized steaks into the flour, then the buttermilk, and then the breadcrumb mixture, pressing the crumbs onto the steak. Place them on a baking sheet and spray both sides generously with vegetable or canola oil.
3. Preheat the air fryer to 400°F.
4. Transfer the steaks to the air fryer basket, two at a time, and air-fry for 10 minutes, flipping the steaks over halfway through the cooking time. This will cook your steaks to medium. If you want the steaks cooked a little more or less, add or subtract a minute or two. Hold the first batch of steaks warm in a 170°F oven while you cook the second batch.
5. While the steaks are cooking, make the gravy. Melt the butter in a small saucepan over medium heat on the stovetop. Add the onion, garlic and thyme and cook for five minutes, until the onion is soft and just starting to brown. Stir in the flour and cook for another five minutes, stirring regularly, until the mixture starts to brown. Whisk in the milk and bring the mixture to a boil to thicken. Season to taste with salt, lots of freshly ground black pepper and a few dashes of Worcestershire sauce.
6. Plate the chicken fried steaks with mashed potatoes and vegetables and serve the gravy at the table to pour over the top.

Coconut Curry Chicken With Coconut Rice

Servings: 4 / Cooking Time: 56 Mins.

Ingredients:

- 1 (14-ounce) can coconut milk
- 2 tbsp. green or red curry paste
- zest and juice of one lime
- 1 clove garlic, minced
- 1 tbsp. grated fresh ginger
- 1 tsp. ground cumin
- 1 (3- to 4-pound) chicken, cut into 8 pieces
- vegetable or olive oil
- salt and freshly ground black pepper
- fresh cilantro leaves
- For the rice:
- 1 C. basmati or jasmine rice
- 1 C. water
- 1 C. coconut milk
- ½ tsp. salt
- freshly ground black pepper

Directions:

1. Make the marinade by combining the coconut milk, curry paste, lime zest and juice, garlic, ginger and cumin. Coat the chicken on all sides with the marinade and marinate the chicken for 1 hour to overnight in the refrigerator.
2. Preheat the air fryer to 380°F.
3. Brush the bottom of the air fryer basket with oil. Transfer the chicken thighs and drumsticks from the marinade to the air fryer basket, letting most of the marinade drip off. Season to taste with salt and freshly ground black pepper.
4. Air-fry the chicken drumsticks and thighs at 380°F for 12 minutes. Flip the chicken over and continue to air-fry for another 12 minutes. Set aside and air-fry the chicken breast pieces at 380°F for 15 minutes. Turn the chicken breast pieces over and air-fry for another 12 minutes. Return the chicken thighs and drumsticks to the air fryer and air-fry for an additional 5 minutes.
5. While the chicken is cooking, make the coconut rice. Rinse the rice kernels with water and drain well. Place the rice in a medium saucepan with a tight fitting lid, along with the water, coconut milk, salt and freshly ground black pepper. Bring the mixture to a boil and then cover, reduce the heat and let it cook gently for 20 minutes without lifting the lid. When the time is up, lift the lid, fluff with a fork and set aside.
6. Remove the chicken from the air fryer and serve warm with the coconut rice and fresh cilantro scattered around.

Crispy "fried" Chicken

Servings: 4 / Cooking Time: 14 Mins.

Ingredients:

- ¾ C. all-purpose flour
- ½ tsp. paprika
- ¼ tsp. black pepper
- ¼ tsp. salt
- 2 large eggs
- 1½ C. panko breadcrumbs
- 1 lb. boneless, skinless chicken tenders

Directions:

1. Preheat the air fryer to 400°F.
2. In a shallow bowl, mix the flour with the paprika, pepper, and salt.
3. In a separate bowl, whisk the eggs; set aside.
4. In a third bowl, place the breadcrumbs.
5. Liberally spray the air fryer basket with olive oil spray.
6. Pat the chicken tenders dry with a paper towel. Dredge the tenders one at a time in the flour, then dip them in the egg, and toss them in the breadcrumb coating. Repeat until all tenders are coated.
7. Set each tender in the air fryer, leaving room on each side of the tender to allow for flipping.
8. When the basket is full, cook 4 to 7 minutes, flip, and cook another 4 to 7 minutes.
9. Remove the tenders and let cool 5 minutes before serving. Repeat until all tenders are cooked.

Buffalo Egg Rolls

Servings: 8 / Cooking Time: 9 Minutes

Ingredients:

- 1 tsp. water
- 1 tbsp. cornstarch
- 1 egg
- 2½ C. cooked chicken, diced or shredded (see opposite page)
- ⅓ C. chopped green onion
- ⅓ C. diced celery
- ⅓ C. buffalo wing sauce
- 8 egg roll wraps
- oil for misting or cooking spray
- Blue Cheese Dip
- 3 oz. cream cheese, softened
- ⅓ C. blue cheese, crumbled
- 1 tsp. Worcestershire sauce
- ¼ tsp. garlic powder
- ¼ C. buttermilk (or sour cream)

Directions:

1. Mix water and cornstarch in a small bowl until dissolved. Add egg, beat well, and set aside.
2. In a medium size bowl, mix together chicken, green onion, celery, and buffalo wing sauce.
3. Divide chicken mixture evenly among 8 egg roll wraps, spooning ½ inch from one edge.
4. Moisten all edges of each wrap with beaten egg wash.
5. Fold the short ends over filling, then roll up tightly and press to seal edges.
6. Brush outside of wraps with egg wash, then spritz with oil or cooking spray.
7. Place 4 egg rolls in air fryer basket.
8. Cook at 390°F for 9minutes or until outside is brown and crispy.
9. While the rolls are cooking, prepare the Blue Cheese Dip. With a fork, mash together cream cheese and blue cheese.
10. Stir in remaining ingredients.
11. Dip should be just thick enough to slightly cling to egg rolls. If too thick, stir in buttermilk or milk 1 tbsp. at a time until you reach the desired consistency.
12. Cook remaining 4 egg rolls as in steps 7 and 8.
13. Serve while hot with Blue Cheese Dip, more buffalo wing sauce, or both.

Sweet-and-sour Chicken

Servings: 6 / Cooking Time: 10 Mins.

Ingredients:

- 1 C. pineapple juice
- 1 C. plus 3 tbsp. cornstarch, divided
- ¼ C. sugar
- ¼ C. ketchup
- ¼ C. apple cider vinegar
- 2 tbsp. soy sauce or tamari
- 1 tsp. garlic powder, divided
- ¼ C. flour
- 1 tbsp. sesame seeds
- ½ tsp. salt
- ¼ tsp. ground black pepper
- 2 large eggs
- 2 lb. chicken breasts, cut into 1-inch cubes
- 1 red bell pepper, cut into 1-inch pieces
- 1 carrot, sliced into ¼-inch-thick rounds

Directions:

1. In a medium saucepan, whisk together the pineapple juice, 3 tbsp. of the cornstarch, the sugar, the ketchup, the apple cider vinegar, the soy sauce or tamari, and ½ tsp. of the garlic powder. Cook over medium-low heat, whisking occasionally as the sauce thickens, about 6 minutes. Stir and set aside while preparing the chicken.
2. Preheat the air fryer to 370°F.
3. In a medium bowl, place the remaining 1 C. of cornstarch, the flour, the sesame seeds, the salt, the remaining ½ tsp. of garlic powder, and the pepper.
4. In a second medium bowl, whisk the eggs.
5. Working in batches, place the cubed chicken in the cornstarch mixture to lightly coat; then dip it into the egg mixture, and return it to the cornstarch mixture. Shake off the excess and place the coated chicken in the air fryer basket. Spray with cooking spray and cook for 5 minutes, shake the basket, and spray with more cooking spray. Cook an additional 3 to 5 minutes, or until completely cooked and golden brown.
6. On the last batch of chicken, add the bell pepper and carrot to the basket and cook with the chicken.
7. Place the cooked chicken and vegetables into a serving bowl and toss with the sweet-and-sour sauce to serve.

Peachy Chicken Chunks With Cherries

Servings: 4 / Cooking Time: 16 Mins.

Ingredients:

- ⅓ C. peach preserves
- 1 tsp. ground rosemary
- ½ tsp. black pepper
- ½ tsp. salt
- ½ tsp. marjoram
- 1 tsp. light olive oil
- 1 lb. boneless chicken breasts, cut in 1½-inch chunks
- oil for misting or cooking spray
- 10-ounce package frozen unsweetened dark cherries, thawed and drained

Directions:

1. In a medium bowl, mix together peach preserves, rosemary, pepper, salt, marjoram, and olive oil.
2. Stir in chicken chunks and toss to coat well with the preserve mixture.
3. Spray air fryer basket with oil or cooking spray and lay chicken chunks in basket.
4. Cook at 390°F for 7minutes. Stir. Cook for 8 more minutes or until chicken juices run clear.
5. When chicken has cooked through, scatter the cherries over and cook for additional minute to heat cherries.

Quick Chicken For Filling

Servings: 2 / Cooking Time: 8 Mins.

Ingredients:

- 1 lb. chicken tenders, skinless and boneless
- ½ tsp. ground cumin
- ½ tsp. garlic powder
- cooking spray

Directions:

1. Sprinkle raw chicken tenders with seasonings.
2. Spray air fryer basket lightly with cooking spray to prevent sticking.
3. Place chicken in air fryer basket in single layer.
4. Cook at 390°F for 4minutes, turn chicken strips over, and cook for an additional 4minutes.
5. Test for doneness. Thick tenders may require an additional minute or two.

Chicken Cutlets With Broccoli Rabe And Roasted Peppers

Servings: 2 / Cooking Time: 10 Mins.

Ingredients:

- ½ bunch broccoli rabe
- olive oil, in a spray bottle
- salt and freshly ground black pepper
- ⅔ C. roasted red pepper strips
- 2 (4-ounce) boneless, skinless chicken breasts
- 2 tbsp. all-purpose flour
- 1 egg, beaten
- ⅓ C. seasoned breadcrumbs
- 2 slices aged provolone cheese

Directions:

1. Bring a medium saucepot of salted water to a boil on the stovetop. Blanch the broccoli rabe for 3 minutes in the boiling water and then drain. When it has cooled a little, squeeze out as much water as possible, drizzle a little olive oil on top, season with salt and black pepper and set aside. Dry the roasted red peppers with a clean kitchen towel and set them aside as well.
2. Place each chicken breast between 2 pieces of plastic wrap. Use a meat pounder to flatten the chicken breasts to about ½-inch thick. Season the chicken on both sides with salt and pepper.
3. Preheat the air fryer to 400°F.
4. Set up a dredging station with three shallow dishes. Place the flour in one dish, the egg in a second dish and the breadcrumbs in a third dish. Coat the chicken on all sides with the flour. Shake off any excess flour and dip the chicken into the egg. Let the excess egg drip off and coat both sides of the chicken in the breadcrumbs. Spray the chicken with olive oil on both sides and transfer to the air fryer basket.
5. Air-fry the chicken at 400°F for 5 minutes. Turn the chicken over and air-fry for another minute. Then, top the chicken breast with the broccoli rabe and roasted peppers. Place a slice of the provolone cheese on top and secure it with a toothpick or two.
6. Air-fry at 360° for 3 to 4 minutes to melt the cheese and warm everything together.

BEEF, PORK & LAMB RECIPES

Bourbon Bacon Burgers

Servings: 2 / Cooking Time: 23-28 Mins.

Ingredients:

- 1 tbsp. bourbon
- 2 tbsp. brown sugar
- 3 strips maple bacon, cut in half
- ¾ lb. ground beef (80% lean)
- 1 tbsp. minced onion
- 2 tbsp. BBQ sauce
- ½ tsp. salt
- freshly ground black pepper
- 2 slices Colby Jack cheese (or Monterey Jack)
- 2 Kaiser rolls
- lettuce and tomato, for serving
- Zesty Burger Sauce:
- 2 tbsp. BBQ sauce
- 2 tbsp. mayonnaise
- ¼ tsp. ground paprika
- freshly ground black pepper

Directions:

1. Preheat the air fryer to 390°F and pour a little water into the bottom of the air fryer drawer. (This will help prevent the grease that drips into the bottom drawer from burning and smoking.)
2. Combine the bourbon and brown sugar in a small bowl. Place the bacon strips in the air fryer basket and brush with the brown sugar mixture. Air-fry at 390°F for 4 minutes. Flip the bacon over, brush with more brown sugar and air-fry at 390°F for an additional 4 minutes until crispy.
3. While the bacon is cooking, make the burger patties. Combine the ground beef, onion, BBQ sauce, salt and pepper in a large bowl. Mix together thoroughly with your hands and shape the meat into 2 patties.
4. Transfer the burger patties to the air fryer basket and air-fry the burgers at 370°F for 15 to 20 minutes, depending on how you like your burger cooked (15 minutes for rare to medium-rare; 20 minutes for well-done). Flip the burgers over halfway through the cooking process.
5. While the burgers are air-frying, make the burger sauce by combining the BBQ sauce, mayonnaise, paprika and freshly ground black pepper in a bowl.
6. When the burgers are cooked to your liking, top each patty with a slice of Colby Jack cheese and air-fry for an additional minute, just to melt the cheese. (You might want to pin the cheese slice to the burger with a toothpick to prevent it from blowing off in your air fryer.) Spread the sauce on the inside of the Kaiser rolls, place the burgers on the rolls, top with the bourbon bacon, lettuce and tomato and enjoy!

Apple Cornbread Stuffed Pork Loin With Apple Gravy

Servings: 4 / Cooking Time: 61 Mins.

Ingredients:

- 4 strips of bacon, chopped
- 1 Granny Smith apple, peeled, cored and finely chopped
- 2 tsp. fresh thyme leaves
- ¼ C. chopped fresh parsley
- 2 C. cubed cornbread
- ½ C. chicken stock
- salt and freshly ground black pepper
- 1 (2-pound) boneless pork loin
- kitchen twine
- Apple Gravy:
- 2 tbsp. butter
- 1 shallot, minced
- 1 Granny Smith apple, peeled, cored and finely chopped
- 3 sprigs fresh thyme
- 2 tbsp. flour
- 1 C. chicken stock
- ½ C. apple cider
- salt and freshly ground black pepper, to taste

Directions:

1. Preheat the air fryer to 400°F.
2. Add the bacon to the air fryer and air-fry for 6 minutes until crispy. While the bacon is cooking, combine the apple, fresh thyme, parsley and cornbread in a bowl and toss well. Moisten the mixture with the chicken stock and season to taste with salt and freshly ground black pepper. Add the cooked bacon to the mixture.
3. Butterfly the pork loin by holding it flat on the cutting board with one hand, while slicing into the pork loin parallel to the cutting board with the other. Slice into the longest side of the pork loin, but stop before you cut all the way through. You should then be able to open the pork loin up like a book, making it twice as wide as it was when you started. Season the inside of the pork with salt and freshly ground black pepper.
4. Spread the cornbread mixture onto the butterflied pork loin, leaving a one-inch border around the edge of the pork. Roll the pork loin up around the stuffing to enclose the stuffing, and tie the rolled pork in several places with kitchen twine or secure with toothpicks. Try to replace any stuffing that falls out of the roast as you roll it, by stuffing it into the ends of the rolled pork. Season the outside of the pork with salt and freshly ground black pepper.
5. Preheat the air fryer to 360°F.
6. Place the stuffed pork loin into the air fryer, seam side down. Air-fry the pork loin for 15 minutes at 360°F. Turn the pork loin over and air-fry for an additional 15 minutes. Turn the pork loin a quarter turn and air-fry for an additional 15 minutes. Turn the pork loin over again to expose the fourth side, and air-fry for an additional 10 minutes. The pork loin should register 155°F on an instant read thermometer when it is finished.
7. While the pork is cooking, make the apple gravy. Preheat a saucepan over medium heat on the stovetop and melt the butter. Add the shallot, apple and thyme sprigs and sauté until the apple starts to soften and brown a little. Add the flour and stir for a minute or two. Whisk in the stock and apple cider vigorously to prevent the flour from forming lumps. Bring the mixture to a boil to thicken and season to taste with salt and pepper.
8. Transfer the pork loin to a resting plate and loosely tent with foil, letting the pork rest for at least 5 minutes before slicing and serving with the apple gravy poured over the top.

Crispy Five-spice Pork Belly

Servings: 6 / Cooking Time: 60-75 Mins.

Ingredients:

- 1½ lb. Pork belly with skin
- 3 tbsp. Shaoxing (Chinese cooking rice wine), dry sherry, or white grape juice
- 1½ tsp. Granulated white sugar
- ¾ tsp. Five-spice powder (see the headnote)
- 1¼ C. Coarse sea salt or kosher salt

Directions:

1. Preheat the air fryer to 350°F.
2. Set the pork belly skin side up on a cutting board. Use a meat fork to make dozens and dozens of tiny holes all across the surface of the skin. You can hardly make too many holes. These will allow the skin to bubble up and keep it from becoming hard as it roasts.
3. Turn the pork belly over so that one of its longer sides faces you. Make four evenly spaced vertical slits in the meat. The slits should go about halfway into the meat toward the fat.
4. Mix the Shaoxing or its substitute, sugar, and five-spice powder in a small bowl until the sugar dissolves. Massage this mixture across the meat and into the cuts.
5. Turn the pork belly over again. Blot dry any moisture on the skin. Make a double-thickness aluminum foil tray by setting two 10-inch-long pieces of foil on top of another. Set the pork belly skin side up in the center of this tray. Fold the sides of the tray up toward the pork, crimping the foil as you work to make a high-sided case all around the pork belly. Seal the foil to the meat on all sides so that only the skin is exposed.
6. Pour the salt onto the skin and pat it down and in place to create a crust. Pick up the foil tray with the pork in it and set it in the basket.
7. Air-fry undisturbed for 35 minutes for a small batch, 45 minutes for a medium batch, or 50 minutes for a large batch.
8. Remove the foil tray with the pork belly still in it. Warning: The foil tray is full of scalding-hot fat. Discard the fat in the tray (not down the drain!), as well as the tray itself. Transfer the pork belly to a cutting board.
9. Raise the air fryer temperature to 375°F (or 380°F or 390°F, if one of these is the closest setting). Brush the salt crust off the pork, removing any visible salt from the sides of the meat, too.
10. When the machine is at temperature, return the pork belly skin side up to the basket. Air-fry undisturbed for 25 minutes, or until crisp and very well browned. If the machine is at 390°F, you may be able to shave 5 minutes off the cooking time so that the skin doesn't blacken.
11. Use a nonstick-safe spatula, and perhaps a silicone baking mitt, to transfer the pork belly to a wire rack. Cool for 10 minutes before serving.

Albóndigas

Servings: 4 / Cooking Time: 15 Mins.

Ingredients:

- 1 lb. Lean ground pork
- 3 tbsp. Very finely chopped trimmed scallions
- 3 tbsp. Finely chopped fresh cilantro leaves
- 3 tbsp. Plain panko bread crumbs (gluten-free, if a concern)
- 3 tbsp. Dry white wine, dry sherry, or unsweetened apple juice
- 1½ tsp. Minced garlic
- 1¼ tsp. Mild smoked paprika
- ¾ tsp. Dried oregano
- ¾ tsp. Table salt
- ¼ tsp. Ground black pepper
- Olive oil spray

Directions:

1. Preheat the air fryer to 400°F.
2. Mix the ground pork, scallions, cilantro, bread crumbs, wine or its substitute, garlic, smoked paprika, oregano, salt, and pepper in a bowl until the herbs and spices are evenly distributed in the mixture.
3. Lightly coat your clean hands with olive oil spray, then form the ground pork mixture into balls, using 2 tbsp. for each one. Spray your hands frequently so that the meat mixture doesn't stick.
4. Set the balls in the basket so that they're not touching, even if they're close together. Air-fry undisturbed for 15 minutes, or until well browned and an instant-read meat thermometer inserted into one or two balls registers 165°F.
5. Use a nonstick-safe spatula and kitchen tongs for balance to gently transfer the fragile balls to a wire rack to cool for 5 minutes before serving.

Garlic And Oregano Lamb Chops

Servings: 4 / Cooking Time: 17 Mins.

Ingredients:

- 1½ tbsp. Olive oil
- 1 tbsp. Minced garlic
- 1 tsp. Dried oregano
- 1 tsp. Finely minced orange zest
- ¾ tsp. Fennel seeds
- ¾ tsp. Table salt
- ¾ tsp. Ground black pepper
- 6 4-ounce, 1-inch-thick lamb loin chops

Directions:

1. Mix the olive oil, garlic, oregano, orange zest, fennel seeds, salt, and pepper in a large bowl. Add the chops and toss well to coat. Set aside as the air fryer heats, tossing one more time.
2. Preheat the air fryer to 400°F.
3. Set the chops bone side down in the basket (that is, so they stand up on their bony edge) with as much air space between them as possible. Air-fry undisturbed for 14 minutes for medium-rare, or until an instant-read meat thermometer inserted into the thickest part of a chop (without touching bone) registers 132°F (not USDA-approved). Or air-fry undisturbed for 17 minutes for well done, or until an instant-read meat thermometer registers 145°F (USDA-approved).
4. Use kitchen tongs to transfer the chops to a wire rack. Cool for 5 minutes before serving.

T-bone Steak With Roasted Tomato, Corn And Asparagus Salsa

Servings: 2 / Cooking Time: 15-20 Mins.

Ingredients:

- 1 (20-ounce) T-bone steak
- salt and freshly ground black pepper
- Salsa
- 1½ C. cherry tomatoes
- ¾ C. corn kernels (fresh, or frozen and thawed)
- 1½ C. sliced asparagus (1-inch slices) (about ½ bunch)
- 1 tbsp. + 1 tsp. olive oil, divided
- salt and freshly ground black pepper
- 1½ tsp. red wine vinegar
- 3 tbsp. chopped fresh basil
- 1 tbsp. chopped fresh chives

Directions:

1. Preheat the air fryer to 400°F.
2. Season the steak with salt and pepper and air-fry at 400°F for 10 minutes (medium-rare), 12 minutes (medium), or 15 minutes (well-done), flipping the steak once halfway through the cooking time.
3. In the meantime, toss the tomatoes, corn and asparagus in a bowl with a tsp. or so of olive oil, salt and freshly ground black pepper.
4. When the steak has finished cooking, remove it to a cutting board, tent loosely with foil and let it rest. Transfer the vegetables to the air fryer and air-fry at 400°F for 5 minutes, shaking the basket once or twice during the cooking process. Transfer the cooked vegetables back into the bowl and toss with the red wine vinegar, remaining olive oil and fresh herbs.
5. To serve, slice the steak on the bias and serve with some of the salsa on top.

Fried Spam

Servings: 2 / Cooking Time: 12 Mins.

Ingredients:

- ½ C. All-purpose flour or gluten-free all-purpose flour
- 1 Large egg(s)
- 1 tbsp. Wasabi paste
- 1⅓ C. Plain panko bread crumbs (gluten-free, if a concern)
- 4 ½-inch-thick Spam slices
- Vegetable oil spray

Directions:

1. Preheat the air fryer to 400°F.
2. Set up and fill three shallow soup plates or small pie plates on your counter: one for the flour; one for the egg(s), whisked with the wasabi paste until uniform; and one for the bread crumbs.
3. Dip a slice of Spam in the flour, coating both sides. Slip it into the egg mixture and turn to coat on both sides, even along the edges. Let any excess egg mixture slip back into the rest, then set the slice in the bread crumbs. Turn it several times, pressing gently to make an even coating on both sides. Generously coat both sides of the slice with vegetable oil spray. Set aside so you can dip, coat, and spray the remaining slice(s).
4. Set the slices in the basket in a single layer so that they don't touch (even if they're close together). Air-fry undisturbed for 12 minutes, or until very brown and quite crunchy.
5. Use kitchen tongs to transfer the slices to a wire rack. Cool for a minute or two before serving.

Honey Mesquite Pork Chops

Servings: 2 / Cooking Time: 10 Mins.

Ingredients:

- 2 tbsp. mesquite seasoning
- ¼ C. honey
- 1 tbsp. olive oil
- 1 tbsp. water
- freshly ground black pepper
- 2 bone-in center cut pork chops (about 1 pound)

Directions:

1. Whisk the mesquite seasoning, honey, olive oil, water and freshly ground black pepper together in a shallow glass dish. Pierce the chops all over and on both sides with a fork or meat tenderizer. Add the pork chops to the marinade and massage the marinade into the chops. Cover and marinate for 30 minutes.
2. Preheat the air fryer to 330°F.
3. Transfer the pork chops to the air fryer basket and pour half of the marinade over the chops, reserving the remaining marinade. Air-fry the pork chops for 6 minutes. Flip the pork chops over and pour the remaining marinade on top. Air-fry for an additional 3 minutes at 330°F. Then, increase the air fryer temperature to 400°F and air-fry the pork chops for an additional minute.
4. Transfer the pork chops to a serving plate, and let them rest for 5 minutes before serving. If you'd like a sauce for these chops, pour the cooked marinade from the bottom of the air fryer over the top.

Stuffed Pork Chops

Servings: 4 / Cooking Time: 12 Mins.

Ingredients:

- 4 boneless pork chops
- ½ tsp. salt
- ½ tsp. black pepper
- ¼ tsp. paprika
- 1 C. frozen spinach, defrosted and squeezed dry
- 2 cloves garlic, minced
- 2 oz. cream cheese
- ¼ C. grated Parmesan cheese
- 1 tbsp. extra-virgin olive oil

Directions:

1. Pat the pork chops with a paper towel. Make a slit in the side of each pork chop to create a pouch.
2. Season the pork chops with the salt, pepper, and paprika.
3. In a small bowl, mix together the spinach, garlic, cream cheese, and Parmesan cheese.
4. Divide the mixture into fourths and stuff the pork chop pouches. Secure the pouches with toothpicks.
5. Preheat the air fryer to 400°F.
6. Place the stuffed pork chops in the air fryer basket and spray liberally with cooking spray. Cook for 6 minutes, flip and coat with more cooking spray, and cook another 6 minutes. Check to make sure the meat is cooked to an internal temperature of 145°F. Cook the pork chops in batches, as needed.

Lamb Burger With Feta And Olives

Servings: 3 / Cooking Time: 16 Mins.

Ingredients:

- 2 tsp. olive oil
- ⅓ onion, finely chopped
- 1 clove garlic, minced
- 1 lb. ground lamb
- 2 tbsp. fresh parsley, finely chopped
- 1½ tsp. fresh oregano, finely chopped
- ½ C. black olives, finely chopped
- ⅓ C. crumbled feta cheese
- ½ tsp. salt
- freshly ground black pepper
- 4 thick pita breads
- toppings and condiments

Directions:

1. Preheat a medium skillet over medium-high heat on the stovetop. Add the olive oil and cook the onion until tender, but not browned – about 4 to 5 minutes. Add the garlic and cook for another minute. Transfer the onion and garlic to a mixing bowl and add the ground lamb, parsley, oregano, olives, feta cheese, salt and pepper. Gently mix the ingredients together.
2. Divide the mixture into 3 or 4 equal portions and then form the hamburgers, being careful not to over-handle the meat. One good way to do this is to throw the meat back and forth between your hands like a baseball, packing the meat each time you catch it. Flatten the balls into patties, making an indentation in the center of each patty. Flatten the sides of the patties as well to make it easier to fit them into the air fryer basket.
3. Preheat the air fryer to 370°F.
4. If you don't have room for all four burgers, air-fry two or three burgers at a time for 8 minutes at 370°F. Flip the burgers over and air-fry for another 8 minutes. If you cooked your burgers in batches, return the first batch of burgers to the air fryer for the last two minutes of cooking to re-heat. This should give you a medium-well burger. If you'd prefer a medium-rare burger, shorten the cooking time to about 13 minutes. Remove the burgers to a resting plate and let the burgers rest for a few minutes before dressing and serving.
5. While the burgers are resting, toast the pita breads in the air fryer for 2 minutes. Tuck the burgers into the toasted pita breads, or wrap the pitas around the burgers and serve with a tzatziki sauce or some mayonnaise.

Rack Of Lamb With Pistachio Crust

Servings: 2 / Cooking Time: 19 Mins.

Ingredients:

- ½ C. finely chopped pistachios
- 3 tbsp. panko breadcrumbs
- 1 tsp. chopped fresh rosemary
- 2 tsp. chopped fresh oregano
- salt and freshly ground black pepper
- 1 tbsp. olive oil
- 1 rack of lamb, bones trimmed of fat and frenched
- 1 tbsp. Dijon mustard

Directions:

1. Preheat the air fryer to 380°F.
2. Combine the pistachios, breadcrumbs, rosemary, oregano, salt and pepper in a small bowl. Drizzle in the olive oil and stir to combine.
3. Season the rack of lamb with salt and pepper on all sides and transfer it to the air fryer basket with the fat side facing up. Air-fry the lamb for 12 minutes. Remove the lamb from the air fryer and brush the fat side of the lamb rack with the Dijon mustard. Coat the rack with the pistachio mixture, pressing the breadcrumbs onto the lamb with your hands and rolling the bottom of the rack in any of the crumbs that fall off.
4. Return the rack of lamb to the air fryer and air-fry for another 3 to 7 minutes or until an instant read thermometer reads 140°F for medium. Add or subtract a couple of minutes for lamb that is more or less well cooked. (Your time will vary depending on how big the rack of lamb is.)
5. Let the lamb rest for at least 5 minutes. Then, slice into chops and serve.

FISH AND SEAFOOD RECIPES

Blackened Catfish

Servings: 4 / Cooking Time: 8 Mins.

Ingredients:

- 1 tsp. paprika
- 1 tsp. garlic powder
- 1 tsp. onion powder
- 1 tsp. ground dried thyme
- ½ tsp. ground black pepper
- ⅛ tsp. cayenne pepper
- ½ tsp. dried oregano
- ⅛ tsp. crushed red pepper flakes
- 1 lb. catfish filets
- ½ tsp. sea salt
- 2 tbsp. butter, melted
- 1 tbsp. extra-virgin olive oil
- 2 tbsp. chopped parsley
- 1 lemon, cut into wedges

Directions:

1. In a small bowl, stir together the paprika, garlic powder, onion powder, thyme, black pepper, cayenne pepper, oregano, and crushed red pepper flakes.
2. Pat the fish dry with paper towels. Season the filets with sea salt and then coat with the blackening seasoning.
3. In a small bowl, mix together the butter and olive oil and drizzle over the fish filets, flipping them to coat them fully.
4. Preheat the air fryer to 350°F.
5. Place the fish in the air fryer basket and cook for 8 minutes, checking the fish for doneness after 4 minutes. The fish will flake easily when cooked.
6. Remove the fish from the air fryer. Top with chopped parsley and serve with lemon wedges.

Shrimp

Servings: 4 / Cooking Time: 8 Mins.

Ingredients:

- 1 lb. (26–30 count) shrimp, peeled, deveined, and butterflied (last tail section of shell intact)
- Marinade
- 1 5-ounce can evaporated milk
- 2 eggs, beaten
- 2 tbsp. white vinegar
- 1 tbsp. baking powder
- Coating
- 1 C. crushed panko breadcrumbs
- ½ tsp. paprika
- ½ tsp. Old Bay Seasoning
- ¼ tsp. garlic powder
- oil for misting or cooking spray

Directions:

1. Stir together all marinade ingredients until well mixed. Add shrimp and stir to coat. Refrigerate for 1 hour.
2. When ready to cook, preheat air fryer to 390°F.
3. Combine coating ingredients in shallow dish.
4. Remove shrimp from marinade, roll in crumb mixture, and spray with olive oil or cooking spray.
5. Cooking in two batches, place shrimp in air fryer basket in single layer, close but not overlapping. Cook at 390°F for 8 minutes, until light golden brown and crispy.
6. Repeat step 5 to cook remaining shrimp.

Lightened-up Breaded Fish Filets

Servings: 4 / Cooking Time: 10 Mins.

Ingredients:

- ½ C. all-purpose flour
- ½ tsp. cayenne pepper
- 1 tsp. garlic powder
- ½ tsp. black pepper
- ¼ tsp. salt
- 2 eggs, whisked
- 1½ C. panko breadcrumbs
- 1 lb. boneless white fish filets
- 1 C. tartar sauce
- 1 lemon, sliced into wedges

Directions:

1. In a medium bowl, mix the flour, cayenne pepper, garlic powder, pepper, and salt.
2. In a shallow dish, place the eggs.
3. In a third dish, place the breadcrumbs.
4. Cover the fish in the flour, dip them in the egg, and coat them with panko. Repeat until all fish are covered in the breading.
5. Liberally spray the metal trivet that fits inside the air fryer basket with olive oil mist. Place the fish onto the trivet, leaving space between the filets to flip. Cook for 5 minutes, flip the fish, and cook another 5 minutes. Repeat until all the fish is cooked.
6. Serve warm with tartar sauce and lemon wedges.

Quick Shrimp Scampi

Servings: 2 / Cooking Time: 5 Mins.

Ingredients:

- 16 to 20 raw large shrimp, peeled, deveined and tails removed
- ½ C. white wine
- freshly ground black pepper
- ¼ C. + 1 tbsp. butter, divided
- 1 clove garlic, sliced
- 1 tsp. olive oil
- salt, to taste
- juice of ½ lemon, to taste
- ¼ C. chopped fresh parsley

Directions:

1. Start by marinating the shrimp in the white wine and freshly ground black pepper for at least 30 minutes, or as long as 2 hours in the refrigerator.
2. Preheat the air fryer to 400°F.
3. Melt ¼ C. of butter in a small saucepan on the stovetop. Add the garlic and let the butter simmer, but be sure to not let it burn.
4. Pour the shrimp and marinade into the air fryer, letting the marinade drain through to the bottom drawer. Drizzle the olive oil on the shrimp and season well with salt. Air-fry at 400°F for 3 minutes. Turn the shrimp over (don't shake the basket because the marinade will splash around) and pour the garlic butter over the shrimp. Air-fry for another 2 minutes.
5. Remove the shrimp from the air fryer basket and transfer them to a bowl. Squeeze lemon juice over all the shrimp and toss with the chopped parsley and remaining tbsp. of butter. Season to taste with salt and serve immediately.

Horseradish-crusted Salmon Fillets

Servings: 3 / Cooking Time: 8 Mins.

Ingredients:

- ½ C. Fresh bread crumbs (see the headnote)
- 4 tbsp. (¼ cup/½ stick) Butter, melted and cooled
- ¼ C. Jarred prepared white horseradish
- Vegetable oil spray
- 4 6-ounce skin-on salmon fillets (for more information, see here)

Directions:

1. Preheat the air fryer to 400°F.
2. Mix the bread crumbs, butter, and horseradish in a bowl until well combined.
3. Take the basket out of the machine. Generously spray the skin side of each fillet. Pick them up one by one with a nonstick-safe spatula and set them in the basket skin side down with as much air space between them as possible. Divide the bread-crumb mixture between the fillets, coating the top of each fillet with an even layer. Generously coat the bread-crumb mixture with vegetable oil spray.
4. Return the basket to the machine and air-fry undisturbed for 8 minutes, or until the topping has lightly browned and the fish is firm but not hard.
5. Use a nonstick-safe spatula to transfer the salmon fillets to serving plates. Cool for 5 minutes before serving. Because of the butter in the topping, it will stay very hot for quite a while. Take care, especially if you're serving these fillets to children.

Lobster Tails With Lemon Garlic Butter

Servings: 2 / Cooking Time: 5 Mins.

Ingredients:

- 4 oz. unsalted butter
- 1 tbsp. finely chopped lemon zest
- 1 clove garlic, thinly sliced
- 2 (6-ounce) lobster tails
- salt and freshly ground black pepper
- ½ C. white wine
- ½ lemon, sliced
- vegetable oil

Directions:

1. Start by making the lemon garlic butter. Combine the butter, lemon zest and garlic in a small saucepan. Melt and simmer the butter on the stovetop over the lowest possible heat while you prepare the lobster tails.
2. Prepare the lobster tails by cutting down the middle of the top of the shell. Crack the bottom shell by squeezing the sides of the lobster together so that you can access the lobster meat inside. Pull the lobster tail up out of the shell, but leave it attached at the base of the tail. Lay the lobster meat on top of the shell and season with salt and freshly ground black pepper. Pour a little of the lemon garlic butter on top of the lobster meat and transfer the lobster to the refrigerator so that the butter solidifies a little.
3. Pour the white wine into the air fryer drawer and add the lemon slices. Preheat the air fryer to 400°F for 5 minutes.
4. Transfer the lobster tails to the air fryer basket. Air-fry at 370° for 5 minutes, brushing more butter on halfway through cooking. (Add a minute or two if your lobster tail is more than 6-ounces.) Remove and serve with more butter for dipping or drizzling.

Fried Oysters

Servings: 12 / Cooking Time: 8 Mins.

Ingredients:

- 1½ C. All-purpose flour
- 1½ C. Yellow cornmeal
- 1½ tbsp. Cajun dried seasoning blend (for a homemade blend, see here)
- 1¼ cups, plus more if needed Amber beer, pale ale, or IPA
- 12 Large shucked oysters, any liquid drained off
- Vegetable oil spray

Directions:

1. Preheat the air fryer to 400°F.
2. Whisk ⅔ C. of the flour, ½ C. of the cornmeal, and the seasoning blend in a bowl until uniform. Set aside.
3. Whisk the remaining ⅓ C. flour and the remaining ½ C. cornmeal with the beer in a second bowl, adding more beer in dribs and drabs until the mixture is the consistency of pancake batter.
4. Using a fork, dip a shucked oyster in the beer batter, coating it thoroughly. Gently shake off any excess batter, then set the oyster in the dry mixture and turn gently to coat well and evenly. Set the coated oyster on a cutting board and continue dipping and coating the remainder of the oysters.
5. Coat the oysters with vegetable oil spray, then set them in the basket with as much air space between them as possible. Air-fry undisturbed for 8 minutes, or until lightly browned and crisp.
6. Use a nonstick-safe spatula to transfer the oysters to a wire rack. Cool for a couple of minutes before serving.

Salmon Croquettes

Servings: 4 / Cooking Time: 8 Mins.

Ingredients:

- 1 tbsp. oil
- ½ C. breadcrumbs
- 1 14.75-ounce can salmon, drained and all skin and fat removed
- 1 egg, beaten
- ⅓ C. coarsely crushed saltine crackers (about 8 crackers)
- ½ tsp. Old Bay Seasoning
- ½ tsp. onion powder
- ½ tsp. Worcestershire sauce

Directions:

1. Preheat air fryer to 390°F.
2. In a shallow dish, mix oil and breadcrumbs until crumbly.
3. In a large bowl, combine the salmon, egg, cracker crumbs, Old Bay, onion powder, and Worcestershire. Mix well and shape into 8 small patties about ½-inch thick.
4. Gently dip each patty into breadcrumb mixture and turn to coat well on all sides.
5. Cook at 390°F for 8minutes or until outside is crispy and browned.

Blackened Red Snapper

Servings: 4 / Cooking Time: 8 Mins.

Ingredients:

- 1½ tsp. black pepper
- ¼ tsp. thyme
- ¼ tsp. garlic powder
- ⅛ tsp. cayenne pepper
- 1 tsp. olive oil
- 4 4-ounce red snapper fillet portions, skin on
- 4 thin slices lemon
- cooking spray

Directions:

1. Mix the spices and oil together to make a paste. Rub into both sides of the fish.
2. Spray air fryer basket with nonstick cooking spray and lay snapper steaks in basket, skin-side down.
3. Place a lemon slice on each piece of fish.
4. Cook at 390°F for 8 minutes. The fish will not flake when done, but it should be white through the center.

Crab Cakes On A Budget

Servings: 4 / Cooking Time: 12 Mins.

Ingredients:

- 8 oz. imitation crabmeat
- 4 oz. leftover cooked fish (such as cod, pollock, or haddock)
- 2 tbsp. minced green onion
- 2 tbsp. minced celery
- ¾ C. crushed saltine cracker crumbs
- 2 tbsp. light mayonnaise
- 1 tsp. prepared yellow mustard
- 1 tbsp. Worcestershire sauce, plus 2 teaspoons
- 2 tsp. dried parsley flakes
- ½ tsp. dried dill weed, crushed
- ½ tsp. garlic powder
- ½ tsp. Old Bay Seasoning
- ½ C. panko breadcrumbs
- oil for misting or cooking spray

Directions:

1. Use knives or a food processor to finely shred crabmeat and fish.
2. In a large bowl, combine all ingredients except panko and oil. Stir well.
3. Shape into 8 small, fat patties.
4. Carefully roll patties in panko crumbs to coat. Spray both sides with oil or cooking spray.
5. Place patties in air fryer basket and cook at 390°F for 12 minutes or until golden brown and crispy.

Fish Sticks With Tartar Sauce

Servings: 2 / Cooking Time: 6 Mins.

Ingredients:

- 12 oz. cod or flounder
- ½ C. flour
- ½ tsp. paprika
- 1 tsp. salt
- lots of freshly ground black pepper
- 2 eggs, lightly beaten
- 1½ C. panko breadcrumbs
- 1 tsp. salt
- vegetable oil
- Tartar Sauce:
- ¼ C. mayonnaise
- 2 tsp. lemon juice
- 2 tbsp. finely chopped sweet pickles
- salt and freshly ground black pepper

Directions:

1. Cut the fish into ¾-inch wide sticks or strips. Set up a dredging station. Combine the flour, paprika, salt and pepper in a shallow dish. Beat the eggs lightly in a second shallow dish. Finally, mix the breadcrumbs and salt in a third shallow dish. Coat the fish sticks by dipping the fish into the flour, then the egg and finally the breadcrumbs, coating on all sides in each step and pressing the crumbs firmly onto the fish. Place the finished sticks on a plate or baking sheet while you finish all the sticks.
2. Preheat the air fryer to 400°F.
3. Spray the fish sticks with the oil and spray or brush the bottom of the air fryer basket. Place the fish into the basket and air-fry at 400°F for 4 minutes, turn the fish sticks over, and air-fry for another 2 minutes.
4. While the fish is cooking, mix the tartar sauce ingredients together.
5. Serve the fish sticks warm with the tartar sauce and some French fries on the side.

SANDWICHES AND BURGERS RECIPES

Chicken Apple Brie Melt

Servings: 3 / Cooking Time: 13 Mins.

Ingredients:

- 3 5- to 6-ounce boneless skinless chicken breasts
- Vegetable oil spray
- 1½ tsp. Dried herbes de Provence
- 3 oz. Brie, rind removed, thinly sliced
- 6 Thin cored apple slices
- 3 French rolls (gluten-free, if a concern)
- 2 tbsp. Dijon mustard (gluten-free, if a concern)

Directions:

1. Preheat the air fryer to 375°F.
2. Lightly coat all sides of the chicken breasts with vegetable oil spray. Sprinkle the breasts evenly with the herbes de Provence.
3. When the machine is at temperature, set the breasts in the basket and air-fry undisturbed for 10 minutes.
4. Top the chicken breasts with the apple slices, then the cheese. Air-fry undisturbed for 2 minutes, or until the cheese is melty and bubbling.
5. Use a nonstick-safe spatula and kitchen tongs, for balance, to transfer the breasts to a cutting board. Set the rolls in the basket and air-fry for 1 minute to warm through. (Putting them in the machine without splitting them keeps the insides very soft while the outside gets a little crunchy.)
6. Transfer the rolls to the cutting board. Split them open lengthwise, then spread 1 tsp. mustard on each cut side. Set a prepared chicken breast on the bottom of a roll and close with its top, repeating as necessary to make additional sandwiches. Serve warm.

Chicken Saltimbocca Sandwiches

Servings: 3 / Cooking Time: 11 Mins.

Ingredients:

- 3 5- to 6-ounce boneless skinless chicken breasts
- 6 Thin prosciutto slices
- 6 Provolone cheese slices
- 3 Long soft rolls, such as hero, hoagie, or Italian sub rolls (gluten-free, if a concern), split open lengthwise
- 3 tbsp. Pesto, purchased or homemade (see the headnote)

Directions:

1. Preheat the air fryer to 400°F.
2. Wrap each chicken breast with 2 prosciutto slices, spiraling the prosciutto around the breast and overlapping the slices a bit to cover the breast. The prosciutto will stick to the chicken more readily than bacon does.
3. When the machine is at temperature, set the wrapped chicken breasts in the basket and air-fry undisturbed for 10 minutes, or until the prosciutto is frizzled and the chicken is cooked through.
4. Overlap 2 cheese slices on each breast. Air-fry undisturbed for 1 minute, or until melted. Take the basket out of the machine.
5. Smear the insides of the rolls with the pesto, then use kitchen tongs to put a wrapped and cheesy chicken breast in each roll.

Reuben Sandwiches

Servings: 2 / Cooking Time: 11 Mins.

Ingredients:

- ½ lb. Sliced deli corned beef
- 4 tsp. Regular or low-fat mayonnaise (not fat-free)
- 4 Rye bread slices
- 2 tbsp. plus 2 tsp. Russian dressing
- ½ C. Purchased sauerkraut, squeezed by the handful over the sink to get rid of excess moisture
- 2 oz. (2 to 4 slices) Swiss cheese slices (optional)

Directions:

1. Set the corned beef in the basket, slip the basket into the machine, and heat the air fryer to 400°F. Air-fry undisturbed for 3 minutes from the time the basket is put in the machine, just to warm up the meat.
2. Use kitchen tongs to transfer the corned beef to a cutting board. Spread 1 tsp. mayonnaise on one side of each slice of rye bread, rubbing the mayonnaise into the bread with a small flatware knife.
3. Place the bread slices mayonnaise side down on a cutting board. Spread the Russian dressing over the "dry" side of each slice. For one sandwich, top one slice of bread with the corned beef, sauerkraut, and cheese (if using). For two sandwiches, top two slices of bread each with half of the corned beef, sauerkraut, and cheese (if using). Close the sandwiches with the remaining bread, setting it mayonnaise side up on top.
4. Set the sandwich(es) in the basket and air-fry undisturbed for 8 minutes, or until browned and crunchy.
5. Use a nonstick-safe spatula, and perhaps a flatware fork for balance, to transfer the sandwich(es) to a cutting board. Cool for 2 or 3 minutes before slicing in half and serving.

Perfect Burgers

Servings: 3 / Cooking Time: 13 Mins.

Ingredients:

- 1 lb. 2 oz. 90% lean ground beef
- 1½ tbsp. Worcestershire sauce (gluten-free, if a concern)
- ½ tsp. Ground black pepper
- 3 Hamburger buns (gluten-free if a concern), split open

Directions:

1. Preheat the air fryer to 375°F.
2. Gently mix the ground beef, Worcestershire sauce, and pepper in a bowl until well combined but preserving as much of the meat's fibers as possible. Divide this mixture into two 5-inch patties for the small batch, three 5-inch patties for the medium, or four 5-inch patties for the large. Make a thumbprint indentation in the center of each patty, about halfway through the meat.
3. Set the patties in the basket in one layer with some space between them. Air-fry undisturbed for 10 minutes, or until an instant-read meat thermometer inserted into the center of a burger registers 160°F (a medium-well burger). You may need to add 2 minutes cooking time if the air fryer is at 360°F.
4. Use a nonstick-safe spatula, and perhaps a flatware fork for balance, to transfer the burgers to a cutting board. Set the buns cut side down in the basket in one layer (working in batches as necessary) and air-fry undisturbed for 1 minute, to toast a bit and warm up. Serve the burgers in the warm buns.

Provolone Stuffed Meatballs

Servings: 4 / Cooking Time: 12 Mins.

Ingredients:

- 1 tbsp. olive oil
- 1 small onion, very finely chopped
- 1 to 2 cloves garlic, minced
- ¾ lb. ground beef
- ¾ lb. ground pork
- ¾ C. breadcrumbs
- ¼ C. grated Parmesan cheese
- ¼ C. finely chopped fresh parsley (or 1 tbsp. dried parsley)
- ½ tsp. dried oregano
- 1½ tsp. salt
- freshly ground black pepper
- 2 eggs, lightly beaten
- 5 oz. sharp or aged provolone cheese, cut into 1-inch cubes

Directions:

1. Preheat a skillet over medium-high heat. Add the oil and cook the onion and garlic until tender, but not browned.
2. Transfer the onion and garlic to a large bowl and add the beef, pork, breadcrumbs, Parmesan cheese, parsley, oregano, salt, pepper and eggs. Mix well until all the ingredients are combined. Divide the mixture into 12 evenly sized balls. Make one meatball at a time, by pressing a hole in the meatball mixture with your finger and pushing a piece of provolone cheese into the hole. Mold the meat back into a ball, enclosing the cheese.
3. Preheat the air fryer to 380°F.
4. Working in two batches, transfer six of the meatballs to the air fryer basket and air-fry for 12 minutes, shaking the basket and turning the meatballs a couple of times during the cooking process. Repeat with the remaining six meatballs. You can pop the first batch of meatballs into the air fryer for the last two minutes of cooking to re-heat them. Serve warm.

Chicken Spiedies

Servings: 3 / Cooking Time: 12 Mins.

Ingredients:

- 1¼ lb. Boneless skinless chicken thighs, trimmed of any fat blobs and cut into 2-inch pieces
- 3 tbsp. Red wine vinegar
- 2 tbsp. Olive oil
- 2 tbsp. Minced fresh mint leaves
- 2 tbsp. Minced fresh parsley leaves
- 2 tsp. Minced fresh dill fronds
- ¾ tsp. Fennel seeds
- ¾ tsp. Table salt
- Up to a ¼ tsp. Red pepper flakes
- 3 Long soft rolls, such as hero, hoagie, or Italian sub rolls (gluten-free, if a concern), split open lengthwise
- 4½ tbsp. Regular or low-fat mayonnaise (not fat-free; gluten-free, if a concern)
- 1½ tbsp. Distilled white vinegar
- 1½ tsp. Ground black pepper

Directions:

1. Mix the chicken, vinegar, oil, mint, parsley, dill, fennel seeds, salt, and red pepper flakes in a zip-closed plastic bag. Seal, gently massage the marinade ingredients into the meat, and refrigerate for at least 2 hours or up to 6 hours. (Longer than that and the meat can turn rubbery.)
2. Set the plastic bag out on the counter (to make the contents a little less frigid). Preheat the air fryer to 400°F.
3. When the machine is at temperature, use kitchen tongs to set the chicken thighs in the basket (discard any remaining marinade) and air-fry undisturbed for 6 minutes. Turn the thighs over and continue air-frying undisturbed for 6 minutes more, until well browned, cooked through, and even a little crunchy.
4. Dump the contents of the basket onto a wire rack and cool for 2 or 3 minutes. Divide the chicken evenly between the rolls. Whisk the mayonnaise, vinegar, and black pepper in a small bowl until smooth. Drizzle this sauce over the chicken pieces in the rolls.

Mexican Cheeseburgers

Servings: 4 / Cooking Time: 22 Mins.

Ingredients:

- 1¼ lb. ground beef
- ¼ C. finely chopped onion
- ½ C. crushed yellow corn tortilla chips
- 1 (1.25-ounce) packet taco seasoning
- ¼ C. canned diced green chilies
- 1 egg, lightly beaten
- 4 oz. pepper jack cheese, grated
- 4 (12-inch) flour tortillas
- shredded lettuce, sour cream, guacamole, salsa (for topping)

Directions:

1. Combine the ground beef, minced onion, crushed tortilla chips, taco seasoning, green chilies, and egg in a large bowl. Mix thoroughly until combined – your hands are good tools for this. Divide the meat into four equal portions and shape each portion into an oval-shaped burger.
2. Preheat the air fryer to 370°F.
3. Air-fry the burgers for 18 minutes, turning them over halfway through the cooking time. Divide the cheese between the burgers, lower fryer to 340°F and air-fry for an additional 4 minutes to melt the cheese. (This will give you a burger that is medium-well. If you prefer your cheeseburger medium-rare, shorten the cooking time to about 15 minutes and then add the cheese and proceed with the recipe.)
4. While the burgers are cooking, warm the tortillas wrapped in aluminum foil in a 350°F oven, or in a skillet with a little oil over medium-high heat for a couple of minutes. Keep the tortillas warm until the burgers are ready.
5. To assemble the burgers, spread sour cream over three quarters of the tortillas and top each with some shredded lettuce and salsa. Place the Mexican cheeseburgers on the lettuce and top with guacamole. Fold the tortillas around the burger, starting with the bottom and then folding the sides in over the top. (A little sour cream can help hold the seam of the tortilla together.) Serve immediately.

Turkey Burgers

Servings: 3 / Cooking Time: 23 Mins.

Ingredients:

- 1 lb. 2 oz. Ground turkey
- 6 tbsp. Frozen chopped spinach, thawed and squeezed dry
- 3 tbsp. Plain panko bread crumbs (gluten-free, if a concern)
- 1 tbsp. Dijon mustard (gluten-free, if a concern)
- 1½ tsp. Minced garlic
- ¾ tsp. Table salt
- ¾ tsp. Ground black pepper
- Olive oil spray
- 3 Kaiser rolls (gluten-free, if a concern), split open

Directions:

1. Preheat the air fryer to 375°F.
2. Gently mix the ground turkey, spinach, bread crumbs, mustard, garlic, salt, and pepper in a large bowl until well combined, trying to keep some of the fibers of the ground turkey intact. Form into two 5-inch-wide patties for the small batch, three 5-inch patties for the medium batch, or four 5-inch patties for the large. Coat each side of the patties with olive oil spray.
3. Set the patties in in the basket in one layer and air-fry undisturbed for 20 minutes, or until an instant-read meat thermometer inserted into the center of a burger registers 165°F. You may need to add 2 minutes to the cooking time if the air fryer is at 360°F.
4. Use a nonstick-safe spatula, and perhaps a flatware fork for balance, to transfer the burgers to a cutting board. Set the buns cut side down in the basket in one layer (working in batches as necessary) and air-fry for 1 minute, to toast a bit and warm up. Serve the burgers warm in the buns.

Sausage And Pepper Heros

Servings: 3 / Cooking Time: 11 Mins.

Ingredients:

- 3 links (about 9 oz. total) Sweet Italian sausages (gluten-free, if a concern)
- 1½ Medium red or green bell pepper(s), stemmed, cored, and cut into ½-inch-wide strips
- 1 medium Yellow or white onion(s), peeled, halved, and sliced into thin half-moons
- 3 Long soft rolls, such as hero, hoagie, or Italian sub rolls (gluten-free, if a concern), split open lengthwise
- For garnishing Balsamic vinegar
- For garnishing Fresh basil leaves

Directions:

1. Preheat the air fryer to 400°F.
2. When the machine is at temperature, set the sausage links in the basket in one layer and air-fry undisturbed for 5 minutes.
3. Add the pepper strips and onions. Continue air-frying, tossing and rearranging everything about once every minute, for 5 minutes, or until the sausages are browned and an instant-read meat thermometer inserted into one of the links registers 160°F.
4. Use a nonstick-safe spatula and kitchen tongs to transfer the sausages and vegetables to a cutting board. Set the rolls cut side down in the basket in one layer (working in batches as necessary) and air-fry undisturbed for 1 minute, to toast the rolls a bit and warm them up. Set 1 sausage with some pepper strips and onions in each warm roll, sprinkle balsamic vinegar over the sandwich fillings, and garnish with basil leaves.

Thai-style Pork Sliders

Servings: 4 / Cooking Time: 15 Mins.

Ingredients:

- 11 oz. Ground pork
- 2½ tbsp. Very thinly sliced scallions, white and green parts
- 4 tsp. Minced peeled fresh ginger
- 2½ tsp. Fish sauce (gluten-free, if a concern)
- 2 tsp. Thai curry paste (see the headnote; gluten-free, if a concern)
- 2 tsp. Light brown sugar
- ¾ tsp. Ground black pepper
- 4 Slider buns (gluten-free, if a concern)

Directions:

1. Preheat the air fryer to 375°F.
2. Gently mix the pork, scallions, ginger, fish sauce, curry paste, brown sugar, and black pepper in a bowl until well combined. With clean, wet hands, form about ⅓ C. of the pork mixture into a slider about 2½ inches in diameter. Repeat until you use up all the meat—3 sliders for the small batch, 4 for the medium, and 6 for the large. (Keep wetting your hands to help the patties adhere.)
3. When the machine is at temperature, set the sliders in the basket in one layer. Air-fry undisturbed for 14 minutes, or until the sliders are golden brown and caramelized at their edges and an instant-read meat thermometer inserted into the center of a slider registers 160°F.
4. Use a nonstick-safe spatula, and perhaps a flatware fork for balance, to transfer the sliders to a cutting board. Set the buns cut side down in the basket in one layer (working in batches as necessary) and air-fry undisturbed for 1 minute, to toast a bit and warm up. Serve the sliders warm in the buns.

Salmon Burgers

Servings: 3 / Cooking Time: 8 Mins.

Ingredients:

- 1 lb. 2 oz. Skinless salmon fillet, preferably fattier Atlantic salmon
- 1½ tbsp. Minced chives or the green part of a scallion
- ½ C. Plain panko bread crumbs (gluten-free, if a concern)
- 1½ tsp. Dijon mustard (gluten-free, if a concern)
- 1½ tsp. Drained and rinsed capers, minced
- 1½ tsp. Lemon juice
- ¼ tsp. Table salt
- ¼ tsp. Ground black pepper
- Vegetable oil spray

Directions:

1. Preheat the air fryer to 375°F.
2. Cut the salmon into pieces that will fit in a food processor. Cover and pulse until coarsely chopped. Add the chives and pulse to combine, until the fish is ground but not a paste. Scrape down and remove the blade. Scrape the salmon mixture into a bowl. Add the bread crumbs, mustard, capers, lemon juice, salt, and pepper. Stir gently until well combined.
3. Use clean and dry hands to form the mixture into two 5-inch patties for a small batch, three 5-inch patties for a medium batch, or four 5-inch patties for a large one.
4. Coat both sides of each patty with vegetable oil spray. Set them in the basket in one layer and air-fry undisturbed for 8 minutes, or until browned and an instant-read meat thermometer inserted into the center of a burger registers 145°F.
5. Use a nonstick-safe spatula, and perhaps a flatware fork for balance, to transfer the burgers to a wire rack. Cool for 2 or 3 minutes before serving.

APPETIZERS AND SNACKS

Spinach Cups

Servings: 30 / Cooking Time: 5 Mins.

Ingredients:

- 1 6-ounce can crabmeat, drained to yield ⅓ C. meat
- ¼ C. frozen spinach, thawed, drained, and chopped
- 1 clove garlic, minced
- ½ C. grated Parmesan cheese
- 3 tbsp. plain yogurt
- ¼ tsp. lemon juice
- ½ tsp. Worcestershire sauce
- 30 mini phyllo shells (2 boxes of 15 each), thawed
- cooking spray

Directions:

1. Remove any bits of shell that might remain in the crabmeat.
2. Mix crabmeat, spinach, garlic, and cheese together.
3. Stir in the yogurt, lemon juice, and Worcestershire sauce and mix well.
4. Spoon a tsp. of filling into each phyllo shell.
5. Spray air fryer basket and arrange half the shells in the basket.
6. Cook at 390°F for 5minutes.
7. Repeat with remaining shells.

Green Olive And Mushroom Tapenade

Servings: 1 / Cooking Time: 10 Mins.

Ingredients:

- ¾ lb. Brown or Baby Bella mushrooms, sliced
- 1½ C. (about ½ pound) Pitted green olives
- 3 tbsp. Olive oil
- 1½ tbsp. Fresh oregano leaves, loosely packed
- ¼ tsp. Ground black pepper

Directions:

1. Preheat the air fryer to 400°F.
2. When the machine is at temperature, arrange the mushroom slices in as close to an even layer as possible in the basket. They will overlap and even stack on top of each other.
3. Air-fry for 10 minutes, tossing the basket and rearranging the mushrooms every 2 minutes, until shriveled but with still-noticeable moisture.
4. Pour the mushrooms into a food processor. Add the olives, olive oil, oregano leaves, and pepper. Cover and process until grainy, not too much, just not fully smooth for better texture, stopping the machine at least once to scrape down the inside of the canister. Scrape the tapenade into a bowl and serve warm, or cover and refrigerate for up to 4 days. (The tapenade will taste better if it comes back to room temperature before serving.)

Pita Chips

Servings: 4 / Cooking Time: 10 Mins.

Ingredients:

- 2 rounds Pocketless pita bread
- Olive oil spray or any flavor spray you prefer, even coconut oil spray
- Up to 1 tsp. Fine sea salt, garlic salt, onion salt, or other flavored salt

Directions:

1. Preheat the air fryer to 400°F.
2. Lightly coat the pita round(s) on both sides with olive oil spray, then lightly sprinkle each side with salt.
3. Cut each coated pita round into 8 even wedges. Lay these in the basket in as close to a single even layer as possible. Many will overlap or even be on top of each other, depending on the exact size of your machine.
4. Air-fry for 6 minutes, shaking the basket and rearranging the wedges at the 4-minute marks, until the wedges are crisp and brown. Turn them out onto a wire rack to cool a few minutes or to room temperature before digging in.

Okra Chips

Servings: 4 / Cooking Time: 16 Mins.

Ingredients:

- 1¼ lb. Thin fresh okra pods, cut into 1-inch pieces
- 1½ tbsp. Vegetable or canola oil
- ¾ tsp. Coarse sea salt or kosher salt

Directions:

1. Preheat the air fryer to 400°F.
2. Toss the okra, oil, and salt in a large bowl until the pieces are well and evenly coated.
3. When the machine is at temperature, pour the contents of the bowl into the basket. Air-fry, tossing several times, for 16 minutes, or until crisp and quite brown (maybe even a little blackened on the thin bits).
4. Pour the contents of the basket onto a wire rack. Cool for a couple of minutes before serving.

Vegetable Spring Rolls

Servings: 6 / Cooking Time: 8 Mins.

Ingredients:

- ¾ C. (a little more than 2½ ounces) Fresh bean sprouts
- 6 tbsp. Shredded carrots
- 6 tbsp. Slivered, drained, sliced canned bamboo shoots
- 1½ tbsp. Regular or low-sodium soy sauce or gluten-free tamari sauce
- 1½ tsp. Granulated white sugar
- 1½ tsp. Toasted sesame oil
- 6 Spring roll wrappers (gluten-free, if a concern)
- 1 Large egg, well beaten
- Vegetable oil spray

Directions:

1. Gently stir the bean sprouts, carrots, bamboo shoots, soy or tamari sauce, sugar, and oil in a large bowl until the vegetables are evenly coated. Set aside at room temperature for 10 to 15 minutes.
2. Preheat the air fryer to 400°F.
3. Set a spring roll wrapper on a clean, dry work surface. Pick up about ¼ C. of the vegetable mixture and gently squeeze it in your clean hand to release most of the liquid. Set this bundle of vegetables along one edge of the wrapper.
4. Fold two opposing sides (at right angles to the filling) up and over the filling, concealing part of it and making a folded-over border down two sides of the wrapper. Brush the top half of the wrapper (including the folded parts) with beaten egg so it will seal when you roll it closed.
5. Starting with the side nearest the filling, roll the wrapper closed, working to make a tight fit, eliminating as much air as possible from inside the wrapper. Set it aside seam side down and continue making more filled rolls using the same techniques.
6. Lightly coat all the sealed rolls with vegetable oil spray on all sides. Set them seam side down in the basket and air-fry undisturbed for 8 minutes, or until golden brown and very crisp.
7. Use a nonstick-safe spatula and a flatware fork for balance to transfer the rolls to a wire rack. Cool for at least 5 minutes or up to 15 minutes before serving.

Beet Chips

Servings: 4 / Cooking Time: 20 Mins.

Ingredients:

- 2 large red beets, washed and skinned
- 1 tbsp. avocado oil
- ¼ tsp. salt

Directions:

1. Preheat the air fryer to 330°F.
2. Using a mandolin or sharp knife, slice the beets in ⅛-inch slices. Place them in a bowl of water and let them soak for 30 minutes. Drain the water and pat the beets dry with a paper towel or kitchen cloth.
3. In a medium bowl, toss the beets with avocado oil and sprinkle them with salt.
4. Lightly spray the air fryer basket with olive oil mist and place the beet chips into the basket. To allow for even cooking, don't overlap the beets; cook in batches if necessary.
5. Cook the beet chips 15 to 20 minutes, shaking the basket every 5 minutes, until the outer edges of the beets begin to flip up like a chip. Remove from the basket and serve warm. Repeat with the remaining chips until they're all cooked.

Onion Ring Nachos

Servings: 3 / Cooking Time: 8 Mins.

Ingredients:

- ¾ lb. Frozen breaded (not battered) onion rings (do not thaw)
- 1½ C. (about 6 ounces) Shredded Cheddar, Monterey Jack, or Swiss cheese, or a purchased Tex-Mex blend
- Up to 12 Pickled jalapeño rings

Directions:

1. Preheat the air fryer to 400°F.
2. When the machine is at temperature, spread the onion rings in the basket in a fairly even layer. Air-fry undisturbed for 6 minutes, or until crisp. Remove the basket from the machine.
3. Cut a circle of parchment paper to line a 6-inch round cake pan for a small air fryer, a 7-inch round cake pan for a medium air fryer, or an 8-inch round cake pan for a large machine.
4. Pour the onion rings into a fairly even layer in the cake pan, then sprinkle the cheese evenly over them. Dot with the jalapeño rings.
5. Set the pan in the basket and air-fry undisturbed for 2 minutes, until the cheese has melted and is bubbling.
6. Remove the pan from the basket. Cool for 5 minutes before serving.

Asian Five-spice Wings

Servings: 4 / Cooking Time: 15 Mins.

Ingredients:

- 2 lb. chicken wings
- ½ C. Asian-style salad dressing
- 2 tbsp. Chinese five-spice powder

Directions:

1. Cut off wing tips and discard or freeze for stock. Cut remaining wing pieces in two at the joint.
2. Place wing pieces in a large sealable plastic bag. Pour in the Asian dressing, seal bag, and massage the marinade into the wings until well coated. Refrigerate for at least an hour.
3. Remove wings from bag, drain off excess marinade, and place wings in air fryer basket.
4. Cook at 360°F for 15minutes or until juices run clear. About halfway through cooking time, shake the basket or stir wings for more even cooking.
5. Transfer cooked wings to plate in a single layer. Sprinkle half of the Chinese five-spice powder on the wings, turn, and sprinkle other side with remaining seasoning.

Crabby Fries

Servings: 2 / Cooking Time: 30 Mins.

Ingredients:

- 2 to 3 large russet potatoes, peeled and cut into ½-inch sticks
- 2 tbsp. vegetable oil
- 2 tbsp. butter
- 2 tbsp. flour
- 1 to 1½ C. milk
- ½ C. grated white Cheddar cheese
- pinch of nutmeg
- ½ tsp. salt
- freshly ground black pepper
- 1 tbsp. Old Bay® Seasoning

Directions:

1. Bring a large saucepan of salted water to a boil on the stovetop while you peel and cut the potatoes. Blanch the potatoes in the boiling salted water for 4 minutes while you Preheat the air fryer to 400°F. Strain the potatoes and rinse them with cold water. Dry them well with a clean kitchen towel.
2. Toss the dried potato sticks gently with the oil and place them in the air fryer basket. Air-fry for 25 minutes, shaking the basket a few times while the fries cook to help them brown evenly.
3. While the fries are cooking, melt the butter in a medium saucepan. Whisk in the flour and cook for one minute. Slowly add 1 C. of milk, whisking constantly. Bring the mixture to a simmer and continue to whisk until it thickens. Remove the pan from the heat and stir in the Cheddar cheese. Add a pinch of nutmeg and season with salt and freshly ground black pepper. Transfer the warm cheese sauce to a serving dish. Thin with more milk if you want the sauce a little thinner.
4. As soon as the French fries have finished air-frying transfer them to a large bowl and season them with the Old Bay® Seasoning. Return the fries to the air fryer basket and air-fry for an additional 3 to 5 minutes. Serve immediately with the warm white Cheddar cheese sauce.

Grilled Ham & Muenster Cheese On Raisin Bread

Servings: 1 / Cooking Time: 10 Mins.

Ingredients:

- 2 slices raisin bread
- 2 tbsp. butter, softened
- 2 tsp. honey mustard
- 3 slices thinly sliced honey ham (about 3 ounces)
- 4 slices Muenster cheese (about 3 ounces)
- 2 toothpicks

Directions:

1. Preheat the air fryer to 370°F.
2. Spread the softened butter on one side of both slices of raisin bread and place the bread, buttered side down on the counter. Spread the honey mustard on the other side of each slice of bread. Layer 2 slices of cheese, the ham and the remaining 2 slices of cheese on one slice of bread and top with the other slice of bread. Remember to leave the buttered side of the bread on the outside.
3. Transfer the sandwich to the air fryer basket and secure the sandwich with toothpicks.
4. Air-fry at 370°F for 5 minutes. Flip the sandwich over, remove the toothpicks and air-fry for another 5 minutes. Cut the sandwich in half and enjoy!!

Shrimp Pirogues

Servings: 8 / Cooking Time: 5 Mins.

Ingredients:

- 12 oz. small, peeled, and deveined raw shrimp
- 3 oz. cream cheese, room temperature
- 2 tbsp. plain yogurt
- 1 tsp. lemon juice
- 1 tsp. dried dill weed, crushed
- salt
- 4 small hothouse cucumbers, each approximately 6 inches long

Directions:

1. Pour 4 tbsp. water in bottom of air fryer drawer.
2. Place shrimp in air fryer basket in single layer and cook at 390°F for 5 minutes, just until done. Watch carefully because shrimp cooks quickly, and overcooking makes it tough.
3. Chop shrimp into small pieces, no larger than ½ inch. Refrigerate while mixing the remaining ingredients.
4. With a fork, mash and whip the cream cheese until smooth.
5. Stir in the yogurt and beat until smooth. Stir in lemon juice, dill weed, and chopped shrimp.
6. Taste for seasoning. If needed, add ¼ to ½ tsp. salt to suit your taste.
7. Store in refrigerator until serving time.
8. When ready to serve, wash and dry cucumbers and split them lengthwise. Scoop out the seeds and turn cucumbers upside down on paper towels to drain for 10minutes.
9. Just before filling, wipe centers of cucumbers dry. Spoon the shrimp mixture into the pirogues and cut in half crosswise. Serve immediately.

VEGETARIANS RECIPES

Quinoa Burgers With Feta Cheese And Dill

Servings: 6 / Cooking Time: 10 Mins.

Ingredients:

- 1 C. quinoa (red, white or multi-colored)
- 1½ C. water
- 1 tsp. salt
- freshly ground black pepper
- 1½ C. rolled oats
- 3 eggs, lightly beaten
- ¼ C. minced white onion
- ½ C. crumbled feta cheese
- ¼ C. chopped fresh dill
- salt and freshly ground black pepper
- vegetable or canola oil, in a spray bottle
- whole-wheat hamburger buns (or gluten-free hamburger buns)
- arugula
- tomato, sliced
- red onion, sliced
- mayonnaise

Directions:

1. Make the quinoa: Rinse the quinoa in cold water in a saucepan, swirling it with your hand until any dry husks rise to the surface. Drain the quinoa as well as you can and then put the saucepan on the stovetop to dry and toast the quinoa. Turn the heat to medium-high and shake the pan regularly until you see the quinoa moving easily and can hear the seeds moving in the pan, indicating that they are dry. Add the water, salt and pepper. Bring the liquid to a boil and then reduce the heat to low or medium-low. You should see just a few bubbles, not a boil. Cover with a lid, leaving it askew and simmer for 20 minutes. Turn the heat off and fluff the quinoa with a fork. If there's any liquid left in the bottom of the pot, place it back on the burner for another 3 minutes or so. Spread the cooked quinoa out on a sheet pan to cool.
2. Combine the room temperature quinoa in a large bowl with the oats, eggs, onion, cheese and dill. Season with salt and pepper and mix well (remember that feta cheese is salty). Shape the mixture into 6 patties with flat sides (so they fit more easily into the air fryer). Add a little water or a few more rolled oats if necessary to get the mixture to be the right consistency to make patties.
3. Preheat the air-fryer to 400°F.
4. Spray both sides of the patties generously with oil and transfer them to the air fryer basket in one layer (you will probably have to cook these burgers in batches, depending on the size of your air fryer). Air-fry each batch at 400°F for 10 minutes, flipping the burgers over halfway through the cooking time.
5. Build your burger on the whole-wheat hamburger buns with arugula, tomato, red onion and mayonnaise.

Black Bean Empanadas

Servings: 12 / Cooking Time: 35 Mins.

Ingredients:

- 1½ C. all-purpose flour
- 1 C. whole-wheat flour
- 1 tsp. salt
- ½ C. cold unsalted butter
- 1 egg
- ½ C. milk
- One 14.5-ounce can black beans, drained and rinsed
- ¼ C. chopped cilantro
- 1 C. shredded purple cabbage
- 1 C. shredded Monterey jack cheese
- ¼ C. salsa

Directions:

1. In a food processor, place the all-purpose flour, whole-wheat flour, salt, and butter into processor and process for 2 minutes, scraping down the sides of the food processor every 30 seconds. Add in the egg and blend for 30 seconds. Using the pulse button, add in the milk 1 tbsp. at a time, or until dough is moist enough to handle and be rolled into a ball. Let the dough rest at room temperature for 30 minutes.
2. Meanwhile, in a large bowl, mix together the black beans, cilantro, cabbage, Monterey Jack cheese, and salsa.
3. On a floured surface, cut the dough in half; then form a ball and cut each ball into 6 equal pieces, totaling 12 equal pieces. Work with one piece at a time, and cover the remaining dough with a towel.
4. Roll out a piece of dough into a 6-inch round, much like a tortilla, ¼ inch thick. Place 4 tbsp. of filling in the center of the round, and fold over to form a half-circle. Using a fork, crimp the edges together and pierce the top for air holes. Repeat with the remaining dough and filling.
5. Preheat the air fryer to 350°F.
6. Working in batches, place 3 to 4 empanadas in the air fryer basket and spray with cooking spray. Cook for 4 minutes, flip over the empanadas and spray with cooking spray, and cook another 4 minutes.

Tandoori Paneer Naan Pizza

Servings: 4 / Cooking Time: 10 Mins.

Ingredients:

- 6 tbsp. plain Greek yogurt, divided
- 1¼ tsp. garam marsala, divided
- ½ tsp. turmeric, divided
- ¼ tsp. garlic powder
- ½ tsp. paprika, divided
- ½ tsp. black pepper, divided
- 3 oz. paneer, cut into small cubes
- 1 tbsp. extra-virgin olive oil
- 2 tsp. minced garlic
- 4 C. baby spinach
- 2 tbsp. marinara sauce
- ¼ tsp. salt
- 2 plain naan breads (approximately 6 inches in diameter)
- ½ C. shredded part-skim mozzarella cheese

Directions:

1. Preheat the air fryer to 350°F.
2. In a small bowl, mix 2 tbsp. of the yogurt, ½ tsp. of the garam marsala, ¼ tsp. of the turmeric, the garlic powder, ¼ tsp. of the paprika, and ¼ tsp. of the black pepper. Toss the paneer cubes in the mixture and let marinate for at least an hour.
3. Meanwhile, in a pan, heat the olive oil over medium heat. Add in the minced garlic and sauté for 1 minute. Stir in the spinach and begin to cook until it wilts. Add in the remaining 4 tbsp. of yogurt and the marinara sauce. Stir in the remaining ¾ tsp. of garam masala, the remaining ¼ tsp. of turmeric, the remaining ¼ tsp. of paprika, the remaining ¼ tsp. of black pepper, and the salt. Let simmer a minute or two, and then remove from the heat.
4. Equally divide the spinach mixture amongst the two naan breads. Place 1½ oz. of the marinated paneer on each naan.
5. Liberally spray the air fryer basket with olive oil mist.
6. Use a spatula to pick up one naan and place it in the air fryer basket.
7. Cook for 4 minutes, open the basket and sprinkle ¼ C. of mozzarella cheese on top, and cook another 4 minutes.
8. Remove from the air fryer and repeat with the remaining naan.
9. Serve warm.

Pinto Taquitos

Servings: 4 / Cooking Time: 8 Mins.

Ingredients:

- 12 corn tortillas (6- to 7-inch size)
- Filling
- ½ C. refried pinto beans
- ½ C. grated sharp Cheddar or Pepper Jack cheese
- ¼ C. corn kernels (if frozen, measure after thawing and draining)
- 2 tbsp. chopped green onion
- 2 tbsp. chopped jalapeño pepper (seeds and ribs removed before chopping)
- ½ tsp. lime juice
- ½ tsp. chile powder, plus extra for dusting
- ½ tsp. cumin
- ½ tsp. garlic powder
- oil for misting or cooking spray
- salsa, sour cream, or guacamole for dipping

Directions:

1. Mix together all filling Ingredients.
2. Warm refrigerated tortillas for easier rolling. (Wrap in damp paper towels and microwave for 30 to 60 seconds.)
3. Working with one at a time, place 1 tbsp. of filling on tortilla and roll up. Spray with oil or cooking spray and dust outside with chile powder to taste.
4. Place 6 taquitos in air fryer basket (4 on bottom layer, 2 stacked crosswise on top). Cook at 390°F for 8 minutes, until crispy and brown.
5. Repeat step 4 to cook remaining taquitos.
6. Serve plain or with salsa, sour cream, or guacamole for dipping.

Stuffed Zucchini Boats

Servings: 2 / Cooking Time: 20 Mins.

Ingredients:

- olive oil
- ½ C. onion, finely chopped
- 1 clove garlic, finely minced
- ½ tsp. dried oregano
- ¼ tsp. dried thyme
- ¾ C. couscous
- 1½ C. chicken stock, divided
- 1 tomato, seeds removed and finely chopped
- ½ C. coarsely chopped Kalamata olives
- ½ C. grated Romano cheese
- ¼ C. pine nuts, toasted
- 1 tbsp. chopped fresh parsley
- 1 tsp. salt
- freshly ground black pepper
- 1 egg, beaten
- 1 C. grated mozzarella cheese, divided
- 2 thick zucchini

Directions:

1. Preheat a sauté pan on the stovetop over medium-high heat. Add the olive oil and sauté the onion until it just starts to soften–about 4 minutes. Stir in the garlic, dried oregano and thyme. Add the couscous and sauté for just a minute. Add 1¼ C. of the chicken stock and simmer over low heat for 3 to 5 minutes, until liquid has been absorbed and the couscous is soft. Remove the pan from heat and set it aside to cool slightly.
2. Fluff the couscous and add the tomato, Kalamata olives, Romano cheese, pine nuts, parsley, salt and pepper. Mix well. Add the remaining chicken stock, the egg and ½ C. of the mozzarella cheese. Stir to ensure everything is combined.
3. Cut each zucchini in half lengthwise. Then, trim each half of the zucchini into four 5-inch lengths. (Save the trimmed ends of the zucchini for another use.) Use a spoon to scoop out the center of the zucchini, leaving some flesh around the sides. Brush both sides of the zucchini with olive oil and season the cut side with salt and pepper.
4. Preheat the air fryer to 380°F.
5. Divide the couscous filling between the four zucchini boats. Use your hands to press the filling together and fill the inside of the zucchini. The filling should be mounded into the boats and rounded on top.
6. Transfer the zucchini boats to the air fryer basket and drizzle the stuffed zucchini boats with olive oil. Air-fry for 19 minutes. Then, sprinkle the remaining mozzarella cheese on top of the zucchini, pressing it down onto the filling lightly to prevent it from blowing around in the air fryer. Air-fry for one more minute to melt the cheese. Transfer the finished zucchini boats to a serving platter and garnish with the chopped parsley.

Spaghetti Squash And Kale Fritters With Pomodoro Sauce

Servings: 3 / Cooking Time: 45 Mins.

Ingredients:

- 1½-pound spaghetti squash (about half a large or a whole small squash)
- olive oil
- ½ onion, diced
- ½ red bell pepper, diced
- 2 cloves garlic, minced
- 4 C. coarsely chopped kale
- salt and freshly ground black pepper
- 1 egg
- ⅓ C. breadcrumbs, divided
- ⅓ C. grated Parmesan cheese
- ½ tsp. dried rubbed sage
- pinch nutmeg
- Pomodoro Sauce:
- 2 tbsp. olive oil
- ½ onion, chopped
- 1 to 2 cloves garlic, minced
- 1 (28-ounce) can peeled tomatoes
- ¼ C. red wine
- 1 tsp. Italian seasoning
- 2 tbsp. chopped fresh basil, plus more for garnish
- salt and freshly ground black pepper
- ½ tsp. sugar (optional)

Directions:

1. Preheat the air fryer to 370°F.
2. Cut the spaghetti squash in half lengthwise and remove the seeds. Rub the inside of the squash with olive oil and season with salt and pepper. Place the squash, cut side up, into the air fryer basket and air-fry for 30 minutes, flipping the squash over halfway through the cooking process.
3. While the squash is cooking, Preheat a large sauté pan over medium heat on the stovetop. Add a little olive oil and sauté the onions for 3 minutes, until they start to soften. Add the red pepper and garlic and continue to sauté for an additional 4 minutes. Add the kale and season with salt and pepper. Cook for 2 more minutes, or until the kale is soft. Transfer the mixture to a large bowl and let it cool.
4. While the squash continues to cook, make the Pomodoro sauce. Preheat the large sauté pan again over medium heat on the stovetop. Add the olive oil and sauté the onion and garlic for 2 to 3 minutes, until the onion begins to soften. Crush the canned tomatoes with your hands and add them to the pan along with the red wine and Italian seasoning and simmer for 20 minutes. Add the basil and season to taste with salt, pepper and sugar (if using).
5. When the spaghetti squash has finished cooking, use a fork to scrape the inside flesh of the squash onto a sheet pan. Spread the squash out and let it cool.
6. Once cool, add the spaghetti squash to the kale mixture, along with the egg, breadcrumbs, Parmesan cheese, sage, nutmeg, salt and freshly ground black pepper. Stir to combine well and then divide the mixture into 6 thick portions. You can shape the portions into patties, but I prefer to keep them a little random and unique in shape. Spray or brush the fritters with olive oil.
7. Preheat the air fryer to 370°F.
8. Brush the air fryer basket with a little olive oil and transfer the fritters to the basket. Air-fry the squash and kale fritters at 370°F for 15 minutes, flipping them over halfway through the cooking process.
9. Serve the fritters warm with the Pomodoro sauce spooned over the top or pooled on your plate. Garnish with the fresh basil leaves.

Broccoli Cheddar Stuffed Potatoes

Servings: 2 / Cooking Time: 42 Mins.

Ingredients:

- 2 large russet potatoes, scrubbed
- 1 tbsp. olive oil
- salt and freshly ground black pepper
- 2 tbsp. butter
- ¼ C. sour cream
- 3 tbsp. half-and-half (or milk)
- 1¼ C. grated Cheddar cheese, divided
- ¾ tsp. salt
- freshly ground black pepper
- 1 C. frozen baby broccoli florets, thawed and drained

Directions:

1. Preheat the air fryer to 400°F.
2. Rub the potatoes all over with olive oil and season generously with salt and freshly ground black pepper. Transfer the potatoes into the air fryer basket and air-fry for 30 minutes, turning the potatoes over halfway through the cooking process.
3. Remove the potatoes from the air fryer and let them rest for 5 minutes. Cut a large oval out of the top of both potatoes. Leaving half an inch of potato flesh around the edge of the potato, scoop the inside of the potato out and into a large bowl to prepare the potato filling. Mash the scooped potato filling with a fork and add the butter, sour cream, half-and-half, 1 C. of the grated Cheddar cheese, salt and pepper to taste. Mix well and then fold in the broccoli florets.
4. Stuff the hollowed out potato shells with the potato and broccoli mixture. Mound the filling high in the potatoes – you will have more filling than room in the potato shells.
5. Transfer the stuffed potatoes back to the air fryer basket and air-fry at 360°F for 10 minutes. Sprinkle the remaining Cheddar cheese on top of each stuffed potato, lower the heat to 330°F and air-fry for an additional minute or two to melt cheese.

Lentil Fritters

Servings: 9 / Cooking Time: 12 Mins.

Ingredients:

- 1 C. cooked red lentils
- 1 C. riced cauliflower
- ½ medium zucchini, shredded (about 1 cup)
- ¼ C. finely chopped onion
- ¼ tsp. salt
- ¼ tsp. black pepper
- ½ tsp. garlic powder
- ¼ tsp. paprika
- 1 large egg
- ⅓ C. quinoa flour

Directions:

1. Preheat the air fryer to 370°F.
2. In a large bowl, mix the lentils, cauliflower, zucchini, onion, salt, pepper, garlic powder, and paprika. Mix in the egg and flour until a thick dough forms.
3. Using a large spoon, form the dough into 9 large fritters.
4. Liberally spray the air fryer basket with olive oil. Place the fritters into the basket, leaving space around each fritter so you can flip them.
5. Cook for 6 minutes, flip, and cook another 6 minutes.
6. Remove from the air fryer and repeat with the remaining fritters. Serve warm with desired sauce and sides.

Eggplant Parmesan

Servings: 4 / Cooking Time: 8 Minutes

Ingredients:

- 1 medium eggplant, 6–8 inches long
- salt
- 1 large egg
- 1 tbsp. water
- ⅔ C. panko breadcrumbs
- ⅓ C. grated Parmesan cheese, plus more for serving
- 1 tbsp. Italian seasoning
- ¾ tsp. oregano
- oil for misting or cooking spray
- 1 24-ounce jar marinara sauce
- 8 oz. spaghetti, cooked
- pepper

Directions:

1. Preheat air fryer to 390°F.
2. Leaving peel intact, cut eggplant into 8 round slices about ¾-inch thick. Salt to taste.
3. Beat egg and water in a shallow dish.
4. In another shallow dish, combine panko, Parmesan, Italian seasoning, and oregano.
5. Dip eggplant slices in egg wash and then crumbs, pressing lightly to coat.
6. Mist slices with oil or cooking spray.
7. Place 4 eggplant slices in air fryer basket and cook for 8 minutes, until brown and crispy.
8. While eggplant is cooking, heat marinara sauce.
9. Repeat step 7 to cook remaining eggplant slices.
10. To serve, place cooked spaghetti on plates and top with marinara and eggplant slices. At the table, pass extra Parmesan cheese and freshly ground black pepper.

Veggie Fried Rice

Servings: 4 / Cooking Time: 25 Mins.

Ingredients:

- 1 C. cooked brown rice
- ⅓ C. chopped onion
- ½ C. chopped carrots
- ½ C. chopped bell peppers
- ½ C. chopped broccoli florets
- 3 tbsp. low-sodium soy sauce
- 1 tbsp. sesame oil
- 1 tsp. ground ginger
- 1 tsp. ground garlic powder
- ½ tsp. black pepper
- ⅛ tsp. salt
- 2 large eggs

Directions:

1. Preheat the air fryer to 370°F.
2. In a large bowl, mix together the brown rice, onions, carrots, bell pepper, and broccoli.
3. In a small bowl, whisk together the soy sauce, sesame oil, ginger, garlic powder, pepper, salt, and eggs.
4. Pour the egg mixture into the rice and vegetable mixture and mix together.
5. Liberally spray a 7-inch springform pan (or compatible air fryer dish) with olive oil. Add the rice mixture to the pan and cover with aluminum foil.
6. Place a metal trivet into the air fryer basket and set the pan on top. Cook for 15 minutes. Carefully remove the pan from basket, discard the foil, and mix the rice. Return the rice to the air fryer basket, turning down the temperature to 350°F and cooking another 10 minutes.
7. Remove and let cool 5 minutes. Serve warm.

Veggie Burgers

Servings: 4 / Cooking Time: 15 Mins.

Ingredients:

- 2 cans black beans, rinsed and drained
- ½ C. cooked quinoa
- ½ C. shredded raw sweet potato
- ¼ C. diced red onion
- 2 tsp. ground cumin
- 1 tsp. coriander powder
- ½ tsp. salt
- oil for misting or cooking spray
- 8 slices bread
- suggested toppings: lettuce, tomato, red onion, Pepper Jack cheese, guacamole

Directions:

1. In a medium bowl, mash the beans with a fork.
2. Add the quinoa, sweet potato, onion, cumin, coriander, and salt and mix well with the fork.
3. Shape into 4 patties, each ¾-inch thick.
4. Mist both sides with oil or cooking spray and also mist the basket.
5. Cook at 390°F for 15minutes.
6. Follow the recipe for Toast, Plain & Simple.
7. Pop the veggie burgers back in the air fryer for a minute or two to reheat if necessary.
8. Serve on the toast with your favorite burger toppings.

VEGETABLE SIDE DISHES RECIPES

Curried Cauliflower With Cashews And Yogurt

Servings: 2 / Cooking Time: 12 Mins.

Ingredients:

- 4 C. cauliflower florets (about half a large head)
- 1 tbsp. olive oil
- salt
- 1 tsp. curry powder
- ½ C. toasted, chopped cashews
- Cool Yogurt Drizzle
- ¼ C. plain yogurt
- 2 tbsp. sour cream
- 1 tsp. lemon juice
- pinch cayenne pepper
- salt
- 1 tsp. honey
- 1 tbsp. chopped fresh cilantro, plus leaves for garnish

Directions:

1. Preheat the air fryer to 400°F.
2. Toss the cauliflower florets with the olive oil, salt and curry powder, coating evenly.
3. Transfer the cauliflower to the air fryer basket and air-fry at 400°F for 12 minutes, shaking the basket a couple of times during the cooking process.
4. While the cauliflower is cooking, make the cool yogurt drizzle by combining all ingredients in a bowl.
5. When the cauliflower is cooked to your liking, serve it warm with the cool yogurt either underneath or drizzled over the top. Scatter the cashews and cilantro leaves around.

Roasted Peppers With Balsamic Vinegar And Basil

Servings: 6 / Cooking Time: 12 Mins.

Ingredients:

- 4 Small or medium red or yellow bell peppers
- 3 tbsp. Olive oil
- 1 tbsp. Balsamic vinegar
- Up to 6 Fresh basil leaves, torn up

Directions:

1. Preheat the air fryer to 400°F.
2. When the machine is at temperature, put the peppers in the basket with at least ¼ inch between them. Air-fry undisturbed for 12 minutes, until blistered, even blackened in places.
3. Use kitchen tongs to transfer the peppers to a medium bowl. Cover the bowl with plastic wrap. Set aside at room temperature for 30 minutes.
4. Uncover the bowl and use kitchen tongs to transfer the peppers to a cutting board or work surface. Peel off the filmy exterior skin. If there are blackened bits under it, these can stay on the peppers. Cut off and remove the stem ends. Split open the peppers and discard any seeds and their spongy membranes. Slice the peppers into ½-inch- to 1-inch-wide strips.
5. Put these in a clean bowl and gently toss them with the oil, vinegar, and basil. Serve at once. Or cover and store at room temperature for up to 4 hours or in the refrigerator for up to 5 days.

Rosemary New Potatoes

Servings: 4 / Cooking Time: 6 Mins.

Ingredients:

- 3 large red potatoes (enough to make 3 C. sliced)
- ¼ tsp. ground rosemary
- ¼ tsp. ground thyme
- ⅛ tsp. salt
- ⅛ tsp. ground black pepper
- 2 tsp. extra-light olive oil

Directions:

1. Preheat air fryer to 330°F.
2. Place potatoes in large bowl and sprinkle with rosemary, thyme, salt, and pepper.
3. Stir with a spoon to distribute seasonings evenly.
4. Add oil to potatoes and stir again to coat well.
5. Cook at 330°F for 4minutes. Stir and break apart any that have stuck together.
6. Cook an additional 2 minutes or until fork-tender.

Roasted Garlic And Thyme Tomatoes

Servings: 2 / Cooking Time: 15 Mins.

Ingredients:

- 4 Roma tomatoes
- 1 tbsp. olive oil
- salt and freshly ground black pepper
- 1 clove garlic, minced
- ½ tsp. dried thyme

Directions:

1. Preheat the air fryer to 390°F.
2. Cut the tomatoes in half and scoop out the seeds and any pithy parts with your fingers. Place the tomatoes in a bowl and toss with the olive oil, salt, pepper, garlic and thyme.
3. Transfer the tomatoes to the air fryer, cut side up. Air-fry for 15 minutes. The edges should just start to brown. Let the tomatoes cool to an edible temperature for a few minutes and then use in pastas, on top of crostini, or as an accompaniment to any poultry, meat or fish.

Zucchini Boats With Ham And Cheese

Servings: 4 / Cooking Time: 12 Mins.

Ingredients:

- 2 6-inch-long zucchini
- 2 oz. Thinly sliced deli ham, any rind removed, meat roughly chopped
- 4 Dry-packed sun-dried tomatoes, chopped
- ⅓ C. Purchased pesto
- ¼ C. Packaged mini croutons
- ¼ C. (about 1 ounce) Shredded semi-firm mozzarella cheese

Directions:

1. Preheat the air fryer to 375°F.
2. Split the zucchini in half lengthwise and use a flatware spoon or a serrated grapefruit spoon to scoop out the insides of the halves, leaving at least a ¼-inch border all around the zucchini half. (You can save the scooped out insides to add to soups and stews—or even freeze it for a much later use.)
3. Mix the ham, sun-dried tomatoes, pesto, croutons, and half the cheese in a bowl until well combined. Pack this mixture into the zucchini "shells." Top them with the remaining cheese.
4. Set them stuffing side up in the basket without touching (even a fraction of an inch between them is enough room). Air-fry undisturbed for 12 minutes, or until softened and browned, with the cheese melted on top.
5. Use a nonstick-safe spatula to transfer the zucchini boats stuffing side up on a wire rack. Cool for 5 or 10 minutes before serving.

Sesame Carrots And Sugar Snap Peas

Servings: 4 / Cooking Time: 16 Mins.

Ingredients:

- 1 lb. carrots, peeled sliced on the bias (½-inch slices)
- 1 tsp. olive oil
- salt and freshly ground black pepper
- ⅓ C. honey
- 1 tbsp. sesame oil
- 1 tbsp. soy sauce
- ½ tsp. minced fresh ginger
- 4 oz. sugar snap peas (about 1 cup)
- 1½ tsp. sesame seeds

Directions:

1. Preheat the air fryer to 360°F.
2. Toss the carrots with the olive oil, season with salt and pepper and air-fry for 10 minutes, shaking the basket once or twice during the cooking process.
3. Combine the honey, sesame oil, soy sauce and minced ginger in a large bowl. Add the sugar snap peas and the air-fried carrots to the honey mixture, toss to coat and return everything to the air fryer basket.
4. Turn up the temperature to 400°F and air-fry for an additional 6 minutes, shaking the basket once during the cooking process.
5. Transfer the carrots and sugar snap peas to a serving bowl. Pour the sauce from the bottom of the cooker over the vegetables and sprinkle sesame seeds over top. Serve immediately.

Hawaiian Brown Rice

Servings: 4 / Cooking Time: 12 Mins.

Ingredients:

- ¼ lb. ground sausage
- 1 tsp. butter
- ¼ C. minced onion
- ¼ C. minced bell pepper
- 2 C. cooked brown rice
- 1 8-ounce can crushed pineapple, drained

Directions:

1. Shape sausage into 3 or 4 thin patties. Cook at 390°F for 6 to 8minutes or until well done. Remove from air fryer, drain, and crumble. Set aside.
2. Place butter, onion, and bell pepper in baking pan. Cook at 390°F for 1 minute and stir. Cook 4 minutes longer or just until vegetables are tender.
3. Add sausage, rice, and pineapple to vegetables and stir together.
4. Cook at 390°F for 2 minutes, until heated through.

Fried Cauliflowerwith Parmesan Lemon Dressing

Servings: 2 / Cooking Time: 12 Mins.

Ingredients:

- 4 C. cauliflower florets (about half a large head)
- 1 tbsp. olive oil
- salt and freshly ground black pepper
- 1 tsp. finely chopped lemon zest
- 1 tbsp. fresh lemon juice (about half a lemon)
- ¼ C. grated Parmigiano-Reggiano cheese
- 4 tbsp. extra virgin olive oil
- ¼ tsp. salt
- lots of freshly ground black pepper
- 1 tbsp. chopped fresh parsley

Directions:

1. Preheat the air fryer to 400°F.
2. Toss the cauliflower florets with the olive oil, salt and freshly ground black pepper. Air-fry for 12 minutes, shaking the basket a couple of times during the cooking process.
3. While the cauliflower is frying, make the dressing. Combine the lemon zest, lemon juice, Parmigiano-Reggiano cheese and olive oil in a small bowl. Season with salt and lots of freshly ground black pepper. Stir in the parsley.
4. Turn the fried cauliflower out onto a serving platter and drizzle the dressing over the top.

Chicken Salad With Sunny Citrus Dressing

Servings: 4 / Cooking Time: 8 Mins.

Ingredients:

- Sunny Citrus Dressing
- 1 C. first cold-pressed extra virgin olive oil
- ⅓ C. red wine vinegar
- 2 tbsp. all natural orange marmalade
- 1 tsp. dry mustard
- 1 tsp. ground black pepper
- California Chicken
- 4 large chicken tenders
- 1 tsp. olive oil
- juice of 1 small orange or clementine
- salt and pepper
- ½ tsp. rosemary
- Salad
- 8 C. romaine or leaf lettuce, chopped or torn into bite-size pieces
- 2 clementines or small oranges, peeled and sectioned
- ½ C. dried cranberries
- 4 tbsp. sliced almonds

Directions:

1. In a 2-cup jar or container with lid, combine all dressing ingredients and shake until well blended. Refrigerate for at least 30minutes for flavors to blend.
2. Brush chicken tenders lightly with oil.
3. Drizzle orange juice over chicken.
4. Sprinkle with salt and pepper to taste.
5. Crush the rosemary and sprinkle over chicken.
6. Cook at 390°F for 3minutes, turn over, and cook for an additional 5 minutes or until chicken is tender and juices run clear.
7. When ready to serve, toss lettuce with 2 tbsp. of dressing to coat.
8. Divide lettuce among 4 plates or bowls. Arrange chicken and clementines on top and sprinkle cranberries and almonds. Pass extra dressing at the table.

Brown Rice And Goat Cheese Croquettes

Servings: 3 / Cooking Time: 8 Mins.

Ingredients:

- ¾ C. Water
- 6 tbsp. Raw medium-grain brown rice, such as brown Arborio
- ½ C. Shredded carrot
- ¼ C. Walnut pieces
- 3 tbsp. (about 1½ ounces) Soft goat cheese
- 1 tbsp. Pasteurized egg substitute, such as Egg Beaters (gluten-free, if a concern)
- ¼ tsp. Dried thyme
- ¼ tsp. Table salt
- ¼ tsp. Ground black pepper
- Olive oil spray

Directions:

1. Combine the water, rice, and carrots in a small saucepan set over medium-high heat. Bring to a boil, stirring occasionally. Cover, reduce the heat to very low, and simmer very slowly for 45 minutes, or until the water has been absorbed and the rice is tender. Set aside, covered, for 10 minutes.
2. Scrape the contents of the saucepan into a food processor. Cool for 10 minutes.
3. Preheat the air fryer to 400°F.
4. Put the nuts, cheese, egg substitute, thyme, salt, and pepper into the food processor. Cover and pulse to a coarse paste, stopping the machine at least once to scrape down the inside of the canister.
5. Uncover the food processor; scrape down and remove the blade. Using wet, clean hands, form the mixture into two 4-inch-diameter patties for a small batch, three 4-inch-diameter patties for a medium batch, or four 4-inch-diameter patties for a large one. Generously coat both sides of the patties with olive oil spray.
6. Set the patties in the basket with as much air space between them as possible. Air-fry undisturbed for 8 minutes, or until brown and crisp.
7. Use a nonstick-safe spatula to transfer the croquettes to a wire rack. Cool for 5 minutes before serving.

Hasselback Garlic-and-butter Potatoes

Servings: 3 / Cooking Time: 48 Mins.

Ingredients:

- 3 8-ounce russet potatoes
- 6 Brown button or Baby Bella mushrooms, very thinly sliced
- Olive oil spray
- 3 tbsp. Butter, melted and cooled
- 1 tbsp. Minced garlic
- ¾ tsp. Table salt
- 3 tbsp. (about ½ ounce) Finely grated Parmesan cheese

Directions:

1. Preheat the air fryer to 350°F.
2. Cut slits down the length of each potato, about three-quarters down into the potato and spaced about ¼ inch apart. Wedge a thin mushroom slice in each slit. Generously coat the potatoes on all sides with olive oil spray.
3. When the machine is at temperature, set the potatoes mushroom side up in the basket with as much air space between them as possible. Air-fry undisturbed for 45 minutes, or tender when pricked with a fork.
4. Increase the machine's temperature to 400°F. Use kitchen tongs, and perhaps a flatware fork for balance, to gently transfer the potatoes to a cutting board. Brush each evenly with butter, then sprinkle the minced garlic and salt over them. Sprinkle the cheese evenly over the potatoes.
5. Use those same tongs to gently transfer the potatoes cheese side up to the basket in one layer with some space for air flow between them. Air-fry undisturbed for 3 minutes, or until the cheese has melted and begun to brown.
6. Use those same tongs to gently transfer the potatoes back to the wire rack. Cool for 5 minutes before serving.

Printed in Great Britain
by Amazon

36860459R00064